The Essential

8

Principles of a Strong Family

Sam and Geri Laing

The Essential

8

Principles of a
Strong Family

An Eight-Week Discussion Series for Parents

The Essential 8: Principles of a Strong Family
An Eight-Week Discussion Series for Parents

Copyright © 2013 by Sam and Geri Laing

A special thanks to Amy Morgan for her editorial contributions.

Printed in the United States of America.

ISBN: 978-0-939086-13-6

Unless otherwise indicated, all Scripture references are from the Holy Bible, New International Version, copyright 1973, 1978, 1984, 2011 by the International Bible Society. Used by permission of Zondervan Bible Publishers.

Cover and interior design: Toney C. Mulhollan

About the authors: Sam entered the ministry after earning his BA from the University of Florida in 1971 and since that time has served congregations in Florida, Georgia, Massachusetts, New York and North Carolina. Sam and Geri are presently working with the church in South Florida. They were married in 1972 and have four children, all of whom are faithful Christians. Sam and Geri are also the proud grandparents of ten young grandchildren. The Laings have coauthored three books on marriage and family: *Raising Awesome Kids in Troubled Times–Reloaded*, *Friends and Lovers*, and *The Wonder Years* (with their daughter Elizabeth Thompson). Geri has coauthored with her daughter Elizabeth Thompson *The Tender Years*, a book for the mothers of preschool children. She has also written a book for women, *A Life Worth Living*. Sam has written six other books: *Be Still, My Soul*; *Mighty Man of God*; *The Guilty Soul's Guide to Grace*, *Hot and Holy*, *Warrior*, and *The Warrior Workbook*. Besides their work in Florida, Sam and Geri maintain a busy schedule traveling in the United States and abroad, ministering to churches and conducting seminars on marriage, family and spiritual growth.

Illumination Publishers International
www.ipibooks.com
6010 Pinecreek Ridge Court
Spring, Texas 77379-2513

The Essential 8
Principles of a Strong Family

The First Principle:
First Things First

The Second Principle:
Family Fabric

The Third Principle:
Heart-to-Heart Talks

The Fourth Principle:
Resolve, Repair and Forgive

The Fifth Principle:
Godly Priorities, Sane Schedule

The Sixth Principle:
Church Connection

The Seventh Principle:
Faith, Fun and Laughter

The Eighth Principle:
Family Spirituality

Contents

Contents

Note from the Authors:
When Life Is Not Ideal

Two parents, both in good health, spiritually strong, and deeply in love. Husband and wife married only once, to each other. All the children in the household were born into the family from this marriage.

The description above sounds like a great household—for some of us, it sounds almost too good to be true. Is this the arrangement we need in order to have a great family? Is this the only way it can work? What if our home looks different?

If all of this has to be in place for us to have a "real" family or a strong one, then many of us are in trouble! Certainly there are advantages to being in this situation, but it is oftentimes not the way life turns out.

The good news is this: *The description above is not the only setting in which we can build a thriving family and raise great kids. Strong families can be built in situations that are far from ideal.*

You're not so sure? Let's take a look at some situations and people in the Bible.

- What about the prophet Samuel? He was given over by his parents to be raised by Eli, a man whom God rebuked because he had failed to raise his own two sons with proper discipline and respect for spiritual values. How did little Samuel turn out? *He became Israel's first prophet, the man whose words did not fall to the ground, the man chosen by God to anoint David king over Israel.*

- What about Timothy? His mother and grandmother were faithful

9

Jewish Christians, but his dad was a gentile, and an unbeliever. How did young Timothy turn out? *He became a follower of Jesus and, as a young man, had such character and was so highly regarded by his fellow believers that he was chosen by Paul to be his helper in missionary work. He went on to become a faithful evangelist who was entrusted to lead the church in Ephesus.*

- What about Moses? He was from childhood raised by idol-worshipping Egyptian royalty, while his godly parents had to stand on the sidelines of his life. *He was called by God to lead the Jewish people to freedom and became the great lawgiver of Israel.*

- What about Joseph? His jealous brothers sold him into Egyptian slavery and deceived his father into thinking he was killed by wild animals. He grew up during his teen years as a slave in a pagan household. *He rose from slavery and imprisonment to become Pharaoh's chief assistant. His wisdom and leadership saved Egypt and his estranged family from famine. He kept his faith in God and was eventually reunited and reconciled with his family.*

- What about Esther? Her Jewish name was Hadassah. She was among the captive Jewish remnant enslaved in Persia. Her parents died and her older cousin Mordecai took her in and raised her. She was later taken away and had to become the wife of Xerxes, the Persian king. *She courageously stood up for her people, risking her life to expose and foil a plot to have them slaughtered.*

We share these stories to encourage you that whatever your circumstances, background, or challenges as a parent, *God can and will work in your family.*

God does not confine his blessing and his guidance to only those situations where everything goes smoothly or where families and family members have lived perfectly, or even consistently, with his word or his plan. God is a God of new beginnings. He is a God of redemption. He is a God of the impossible. He is a God who can make a way when there seems to be no way.

Your own family background may have been difficult. You may be a single mother or father trying to raise a family without a spouse to help you. You may be raising children in a family that is full of strife and difficulty, and you are wondering if it is possible for things to ever get better. You may have a spouse who is spiritually indifferent or even in opposition to your faith. You may have divorce in your past. You may have children in your home from other parents and other marriages. You are not only trying to raise them, you are trying to figure out how to build a family out of a group that did not start out together and may not even want to be close.

Take heart, and begin where you are. The good news is that the principles of parenting and raising kids will help in *any* situation. We don't have to feel as if we are doomed to a lesser life or a lesser family just because our situation may be different or fraught with difficulties.

While there is no absolute guarantee in Scripture that even in the best family situations our kids will turn out to be faithful Christians, the Bible does promise that if we put God first, he blesses our lives and is working for our good in all we do (Matthew 6:33; Psalm 127, 128; Romans 8:28). It is far, far better to live faithfully and build our family around spiritual principles than to go the way of the world. Everything we do in a godly direction matters; every effort we make, makes a difference.

Those of us who have family members who are presently spiritually indifferent, astray or rebellious can know that the teaching we have given, the good seed we have sown, and the example we have set will continue to influence them all the days of their lives (Ecclesiastes 11:1–6, Proverbs 22:6, Luke 15:11–24).

So what can we do right now? Let's take on whatever family situation we are in with faith, hope and love. Let's do all we can to be the best parents or grandparents we can be. Whatever time we have to give, let's give it with prayer on our lips, God's word in our hearts and God's priorities in our lives. Let's build a family as best we can with the tools God makes available to us.

I (Sam) lost my father to cancer when I was twelve. I was the youngest of five children, and my two remaining single siblings soon married, leaving my mother and me alone at home. My mom was a believer but was not at that time the committed disciple she later became. When I was fifteen, a faithful uncle paid my way to a church summer camp. I there learned the Scriptures and began going to a Bible-believing church. I later moved away from home to attend college and was there exposed to Jesus' call to discipleship—the call to make him Lord and Savior. After making that decision, God led me to the woman of my dreams and we built our marriage and family as best we could, according to the principles of God's word. Anything good in our life, marriage and family is due to those principles—and to the love and grace of God.

It does not matter how we start, but where we end up. Wherever we may be as parents or as a family, let us faithfully decide, with this program before us, that we will begin right where we are and do all we can to build our family in a way that honors our God and blesses our children.

Introduction:
The Essential 8: Principles of a Strong Family

What is *The Essential 8: Principles of a Strong Family* all about?

Simply put, this is a hands-on workbook to help you get your family on a solid spiritual foundation and keep it there. It is an eight-week plan designed for personal study on a daily basis and in a small discussion group once per week.

We will take you on a journey of discovery of the Essential 8 Principles (E8)—the bedrock concepts you need to understand, believe and implement so as to build a family that is close, spiritual and thriving.

And just who is E8 for?

It is for all parents, from the youngest to the oldest, whether with a spouse or a single parent; from the classic Mom and Dad family to the blended family. The E8 principles are applicable and indispensable in every situation of life.

Yes, much of what we write is directed at the two-parent, spiritually based family. But the principles of family building in this book are not limited to this situation; they are adaptable to others as well.

In that vein, every reader before beginning this journey should study our note, "When Life Is Not Ideal," at the beginning of the book. In it we address how we can adapt our parenting principles and practices to those life situations that can throw us off our game—situations like separation or divorce, or the spiritual decline or disengagement of a marriage partner. Some of us are in blended families or have adopted children—and those situations bring unique challenges. While we cannot do all of these scenarios justice in a book of this scope, we can help you form a mindset to gain what you need to grow a stronger family in whatever situation you face.

Many families in our world are in serious trouble, and countless others, while not in crisis, are far from being strong, spiritual and close. We believe there is a way out and up—a way to a better place and a brighter future. And the good news is, *it's not that complicated!* Who says something has to be complex to be effective and life changing? It is our intention that any parent can understand this material and can, with some persistence over time, see growth in his or her family.

What makes us so sure E8 will work for you? *Because the principles we will share with you come from the Bible*—the ultimate human user manual for life on Planet Earth. God knows what he is doing, and he wants to help us know what we are doing, too! It is our firm belief that following God's word is the only sure way to build a great family. Other plans and programs can supplement, but scriptural principles are the essential foundation without which all the other methods, as brilliant as they may be, cannot succeed.

Some Practical Suggestions

- *Start the Week One Daily Steps* one week <u>before</u> your first discussion group. If you consistently follow this pattern, you will be fully prepared for the discussion each week.
- *Be sure to do the "Daily Steps" every day.* This is the engine that drives the plan forward. We have tried to make the steps fun, simple and doable for busy parents.
- *Fully engage!* Attend a group; read the material. It's only eight weeks long. Hang in there strong to the end, and you will come out on the other side with a solid foundation and a stronger family.
- *Reach out to others for strength.* One of the benefits of this endeavor will be the friendship we can build with other people in our group. We need Jesus the most, but we also need each other. Let's invite and allow others to help us in our family life. Let's form some relationships that can help us to stay strong, encouraged and on track.
- *Don't get overwhelmed.* Building a strong family is a lifelong process, and change takes time. Take on what you can manage, knowing you can always come back and work on some things later.

A stronger family awaits. It's time to get started!

— Sam and Geri Laing

Notes:

_____

_____

_____

_____

_____

_____

_____

_____

_____

_____

_____

_____

_____

_____

_____

_____

_____

_____

_____

_____

_____

_____

_____

_____

_____

_____

_____

Principle 1: **First Things First**

Unless the LORD *builds the house, its builders labor in vain.*

—Psalm 127:1

You are reading this book and embarking on this eight-week journey of learning and growth because you want to build a stronger and better family.

The challenge is great; the needs are immense. Where do we begin?

Sometimes, the task seems beyond human capacity. And, do you know what? You are right. So much so that the only place to start is by turning to God himself. He alone has the wisdom, the understanding, and the means to help us get where we need to go.

Jesus was once asked which of all the commandments in the Bible is the greatest one. His answer was simple, profound and clear:

> *Jesus replied: "'Love the Lord your God with all your heart and with all your soul and with all your mind.' This is the first and greatest commandment. And the second is like it: 'Love your neighbor as yourself.' All the Law and the Prophets hang on these two commandments."*
>
> —Matthew 22:37–40

Our greatest love is to be God himself. He is our greatest passion, our deepest love, our strongest commitment. To build a strong family, God must be first in our lives—before our marriages, our families and ourselves.

Paul said it this way:

When Christ, who is your life, appears, then you also will appear with him in glory.

—Colossians 3:4

I have been crucified with Christ and I no longer live, but Christ lives in me.

—Galatians 2:20

For to me, to live is Christ and to die is gain.

—Philippians 1:21

All of us at one time had something other than "Christ" in this blank: For me to live is _____.

We had words like *job, money, popularity, pleasure, self* or *family* in that blank. What is filling in that blank today? Is it "Christ"?

All of us fall short and have growing to do, but the question is: *What is the most important thing in our life—is Jesus our Lord?*

More than just being good people, more than just being good church members, even more than loving our kids and wanting the best for them—we must make God our number one priority. That is the key to building a strong family.

Most of us made the decision in our past that we would love God first and follow Jesus as our Lord. But here is what can happen: Although we begin with great faith and high resolve, life wears us down. We get distracted. Other things, even important and necessary responsibilities (like raising kids!), can come along and subtly, slowly replace God as our greatest love. Children are one of life's greatest blessings, but we must remember to build our lives on the Giver and not the gifts. God never intended our children to become the center of our existence. He alone is worthy to occupy the place of preeminence in our lives.

When we make the mistake of centering our life on our kids, they are the ones who suffer the most. The thing they most need from us, their parents, is that our lives are devoted to God. That teaches them the right foundation upon which to live.

Our Second Priority

OK, so God is to be our first love. But what, or who, comes next? Who gets second place? Again, we need to turn to the Scriptures for guidance:

> *"Haven't you read," he replied, "that at the beginning the Creator 'made them male and female,' and said, 'For this reason a man will leave his father and mother and be united to his wife, and the two will become one flesh'? So they are no longer two, but one. Therefore what God has joined together, let man not separate."*
>
> —Matthew 19:4–6

Next in line after God comes our husband or our wife. They must be that special person whom we love more than anyone else on earth. More than our love for our children, more than our love for our father or mother or anyone or anything else, our devotion to our spouse must be our greatest earthly love of all.

We start out our married lives deeply in love with our spouse, but when the kids come along, they can start taking up all our time, thought and energy. We start neglecting our marriage. We begin to take each other for granted. Our relationship becomes functional—we no longer have the passion and fire we used to have. And who suffers when we let this happen? You know the answer—the kids!

Next to loving God himself, what our children most need from us is that we are deeply and passionately in love with our spouse.

This is what will give them the security, strength and confidence they need to live successful, victorious lives.

A husband and wife committed to God first and each other second make a powerful team[1]:

---

1. What if you are a single parent, or have a spouse who for whatever reason may not be fully engaged in the parenting process? Do not lose heart! There are many stories in Scripture of children who were successfully raised outside the norm of a two-parent partnership. For example, consider Samuel (1 Samuel 1–3) and Timothy (Acts 16:1–3). Young men like Daniel and Joseph went through the trials of traumatic separation from their families and yet grew up to have exceptional integrity and faith (see Genesis 37, 39 and Daniel 1). God promises that he will make special provision when conditions may be less than ideal (Psalm 27:7–10, Mark 10:29–30).

Two are better than one,
because they have a good return for their work:
If one falls down,
his friend can help him up.
But pity the man who falls
and has no one to help him up!
Also, if two lie down together, they will keep warm.
But how can one keep warm alone?
Though one may be overpowered,
two can defend themselves.
A cord of three strands is not quickly broken.

—Ecclesiastes 4:9–12

So parents, let's summarize:

The most important thing we will ever do for our kids is to love God with the greatest passion of our lives, and to make Jesus our Lord. The next most important thing is to love our spouse more than we love anyone else on earth.

When we have these two priorities in place, we are ready to go. Now we can stand strong. Now we can walk forward. *Now we can build a strong family.*

Group Discussion Questions

- What are your areas of spiritual strength as a disciple and as a parent? Where are you setting a good example for your family? (some examples: personal prayer and Bible study; Christian relationships; church involvement; sharing our faith; personal righteousness)

- Read Luke 8:11–15. In this passage, Jesus describes four kinds of soil, which represent four kinds of people. Where do you see yourself in the parable? Are there changes you need to make?

- What areas are your greatest areas of challenge right now in your spiritual life? Where do you need to renew your commitment?

- Children are one of the greatest gifts God gives us in life. Why do we need to be careful to stay focused on the Giver and not just the gifts he gives us? What happens to our families when our blessings from God—our children, our possessions, our jobs, etc.—become our focus?

- Why does our marriage need to take a greater priority than our kids? What happens to them if we neglect our marriage?

- How is your marriage going? Is it the number two priority in your life?

- Has the addition of children to your marriage hurt or helped your relationship with your spouse? How so?

- If your marriage needs work, what are some ideas to help bring it back to its place of joy, of "first love," that you had when you were newly married?

Read Matthew 18:19–20. Jesus says that when two or more gather in his name, he is right there with them. He also says that when two people ask for something together, it will be done for them.

- What does that tell you about the power of a married couple or a family praying together?

The Power of Prayer to Help Our Families

Let's begin this journey by establishing the habit of prayer in our marriage and family life. Prayer brings God's presence immediately into our midst. It makes God real to us and to our children. It is one of the simplest, easiest and most powerful things we can do to make our families strong. Let's begin praying daily with our spouse. These prayers do not have to be very long—a few sentences spoken to God are powerful! There are times when we need to pray longer prayers, but mostly what we need is daily consistency.

New habits, even simple ones, can be hard to establish. As valuable and transformative as the habit of daily prayer is, it can still be a challenge to get it going. Let's help each other with this. Start looking for another couple in this group you can talk with regularly so that you can encourage each other as you go through these weeks together. We will see God move in powerful ways as we consistently approach him in prayer!

Notes:

_____

_____

_____

_____

_____

_____

_____

_____

_____

_____

_____

_____

_____

_____

_____

_____

_____

_____

_____

_____

_____

_____

_____

_____

_____

_____

_____

_____

_____

My Daily Steps to a Stronger Family

Principle 1: **First Things First**

*Acknowledge and **take to heart this day** that the* Lord *is God in heaven above and on the earth below. There is no other. Keep his decrees and commands, which I am giving you today, so that it may go well with you and your children after you and that you may live long in the land the* Lord *your God gives you for all time.*

—Deuteronomy 4:39–40, emphasis added

Day One (day) _____ (date) _____:

Read Principle 1: **First Things First** Study and Group Discussion Guide.
Read and reflect upon Matthew 22:37–40, Colossians 3:4, Galatians 2:20 and Philippians 1:21.

As stated in the Study Guide, "All of us fall short and have growing to do, but the question is: *What is the most important thing in our life—is Jesus our Lord?*"

Let's do some soul searching here. Think back to the day you made your confession: "Jesus is Lord." Remember the joy you felt and the conviction you had in your mind and heart. Realize that this decision was not only the most important one you ever made but was the most important one you ever made for your family.

- Have you allowed anything to take the place of Jesus in your heart? If so, how has that affected your family?

- Begin today praying for God to renew your "first love" and to fill you with the joy and zeal you had as you began your walk with him—for your sake and for the sake of your family.

Day Two: (day) _____ (date) _____:
Read Psalm 127:1; Deuteronomy 6:1–9.

It is this passage in Deuteronomy that Jesus quotes when he is asked to identify the greatest commandment of all (Matthew 22:37–40).

Note that Moses tells parents what their greatest love in life should be, and then immediately goes on to say that they need to teach this commandment—and all of God's commandments—to their children.

- Why do you think there is such a close connection with parents loving God first and their teaching their children to do the same?
- Moses says the commandments are to be "upon your hearts." Why is this important to us as parents?
- He says we are to "impress" God's commandments on our children. What does that word mean to you?
- According to this passage, in what kinds of settings are we to teach our children God's word? How often? Why is this a more effective way for parents to teach their children than more formal, classroom-type situations?

Day Three: (day) _____ (date) _____:
Read Luke 8:11–15.

In this passage, Jesus identifies four kinds of soil, representing four kinds of people.

- Where do you see yourself in the parable? Are there changes you need to make?
- Think about all this in relationship to your spouse and children. What do they see in your heart, your life and your priorities? If they imitate your example, where will they end up in their spiritual journey?

Day Four: (day) _____ (date) _____:

Read Colossians 3:4; Galatians 2:20; Philippians 1:21.

Time for more soul searching! But let's take a different approach.
Read Revelation 2:1–5.

Jesus calls us to remember the heights of our relationship—those times and
seasons when we were closest to him. Think back to the day of your rebirth,
the day of your baptism into Christ.

- What emotions did you feel that day? Were you relieved? Were you
  excited, exhilarated?

Think back to your early days as a disciple of Christ.

- Did you enjoy your new life? Did you look forward to waking up
  every day, walking with God, reading your Bible, praying, sharing
  your faith and getting to know other disciples?

- Isn't that what God wants you to feel all the days of your life with
  him?

- Continue praying for God to renew your first love, for your sake
  and your family's sake.

Day Five: (day) _____ (date) _____:

Read in Principle 1 the section entitled "Our Second Priority."

- How is your marriage going? Does it have the place of priority in
  your heart that God wants it to have?

- Why is it important for your children to see your devotion, love and
  affection for your spouse? How does this help them?

- What are some things you can do to renew and rekindle this relationship?

Day Six: (day) _____ (date) _____:

Read in Principle 1 the section on "The Power of Prayer to Help Our Families."
Read and reflect upon Matthew 18:19–20; Ecclesiastes 4:9–12.

- Why is prayer between husband and wife so important in building a close, strong marriage and family?

- Why is prayer with your children individually and as a family crucial in building a strong and close family? What does praying together with your children teach them that nothing else does?

Some practical suggestions:

- Begin today to pray daily with your spouse. Don't overwhelm yourself—these prayers do not have to be long, intense or elaborate—consistency is the key! (see Matthew 6:7–8).

- Begin to pray more frequently with your children—not only at meals and bedtime, but also while riding in the car, before leaving for school or work, before going to church—make prayer a natural and "easy" part of your family life, and see what happens!

- You may want to begin to make a "Family Prayer List" of things you are all praying about. As your prayers are answered, give God glory, and watch your family's faith grow.

Day Seven: (day) _____ (date) _____:

Read and meditate upon Joshua 24:14–15.

- What are some decisions and commitments you are making as a husband or a wife, as a father or a mother, to put "first things first"?

_____

_____

_____

- **Special note to husbands and fathers:** As the head of the household, your role is vital. Your passion for loving and serving God should lead the way in your home. *Today, commit to God and to your wife and children that you, like Joshua, will do all you can to lead your family to "serve the Lord."*

Notes:

Principle 2: **Family Fabric**

Every year his parents went to Jerusalem for the Feast of the Passover. When he was twelve years old, they went up to the Feast, according to the custom.

—Luke 2:41–42

He went to Nazareth, where he had been brought up, and on the Sabbath day he went into the synagogue, as was his custom. And he stood up to read.

—Luke 4:16

Because of everything written in this letter and because of what they had seen and what had happened to them, the Jews took it upon themselves to establish the custom that they and their descendants and all who join them should without fail observe these two days every year, in the way prescribed and at the time appointed. These days should be remembered and observed in every generation by every family, and in every province and in every city. And these days of Purim should never cease to be celebrated by the Jews, nor should the memory of them die out among their descendants.

—Esther 9:26–28

If we are to build strong families, we need to weave them tightly together into a beautiful fabric. By "fabric" we mean a structure and a consistent rhythm of events, both ordinary and special, that we build into our family schedules.

For families to be close, they must have regular times when the whole group gets together. During those times we form an identity and feeling that makes us who we are—we become "us"—our own special family that has its unique memories, traditions and customs. It is this kind of togetherness that makes a family close, fun and rich in memory and in feeling.

Your kids will absolutely love the family traditions you build together. They will rely on them. They will learn to count the days until the next celebration, until the next fun family event. They will savor the memories of the past times, and they will plan for and anticipate the future ones.

There is something in human nature that longs for stability, for things we can count on in life. This is why in the Old Testament, God created so many feast days to bring his people together. On those occasions they spent time with each other celebrating their God and their faith. Those feasts were far more than onerous duties; they were the defining events that told God's people, "This is who you are."

While Jesus was opposed to empty, rote obedience that took away the heart of what God wanted these great moments to be, he was not against the events themselves. Far from it—he attended, he joined in, and he called on people to have the right attitude of love, faith and devotion as they participated.

So should we build good and godly habits into our family life. Close families have rhythms and structure to their schedule, and family traditions they honor and enjoy. Ask any close family what their traditions are. Once you get them talking about it, good luck getting them to shut up!

How can we do this in our own families?

Create Habits and Rhythms

We can begin by developing good habits to shape the seemingly inconsequential events of the day. Moments such as waking up, bedtime, bath time...all of them can become a bit enshrined and sanctified with special meaning. Slowing down to take the time to put the little ones to bed at night is a great thing to do. As the kids get older, pausing at bedtime to say good night and share a quiet moment together helps to form memories they will treasure throughout their lives.

Use Mealtimes

We all have to eat, so why not enjoy family meals together? It is amazing what this one simple habit does in building a close family.

Go, eat your food with gladness, and drink your wine with a joyful heart, for it is now that God favors what you do. Always be clothed in white, and always anoint your head with oil. Enjoy life with your wife, whom you love, all the days of this meaningless life that God has given you under the sun.

—Ecclesiastes 9:7–9

There are some interesting interpretation issues in this passage, but the point is that we are meant to enjoy life, enjoy our food, and enjoy each other's company! We strongly encourage you to do your very best to gather the family together for at least one meal per day. This will be the dinner hour for most families. Try not to let family time be eroded by outside forces, especially as school activities increase. Sit down to eat at the same time. Turn off the TV and put away the cell phones. Take off the headsets. No homework or reading the paper at the dinner table. As we used to say to our kids, "Bottom on the chair, feet out front!" And yes, we recommend eating while seated at a table together unless you are having a special pizza movie night like we often did when we "set the floor" and shared a meal picnic-style on a blanket in the family room.

Family dinner conversation is a learned art. Sometimes things may be disjointed and we don't know how to get the family talking together. In our family we would sometimes ask the question, "What did YOU do today?" to everyone at the table. It sounds simple, but we found out what was happening in each other's world, and it kept us close. Over time, we discovered that the kids would actually save up news to share with the family—good grades, a funny or sad story, a tough loss, a great win, an exciting adventure—if it was important to one, it was important to all. Things would get so animated that we had to be sure to help the quieter members of the family to get a word in edgewise. Yes, being a parent takes hard work and careful observation!

Celebrate Birthdays and Holidays

Life gets boring without some special days to sparkle things up. Kids just love those special times—and so do grownups. Even the most grumpy and cranky among us need to loosen up and have some fun! I know some of us grew up without making birthdays, anniversaries and holidays that special. Take another look in your Old Testament. God literally shaped the year of his family, Israel, by their feasts and celebrations. When something awesome happened, they were commanded to commemorate it—they had a meal, they piled up twelve stones—they did something special. The reason? To remind the grownups of and to teach the kids about the great things God had done!

God did mighty deeds in the time of Moses, but the kids who came along later were not there to see the Ten Plagues, eat the first Passover or observe the crossing of the Red Sea. So what did God do? He created a yearly feast to help them remember, and to serve as a teaching opportunity:

> *"When the LORD brings you into the land of the Canaanites, Hittites, Amorites, Hivites and Jebusites—the land he swore to your forefathers to give you, a land flowing with milk and honey—***you are to observe this ceremony*** in this month: For seven days eat bread made without yeast and on the seventh day hold a festival to the LORD. Eat unleavened bread during those seven days; nothing with yeast in it is to be seen among you, nor shall any yeast be seen anywhere within your borders.* **On that day tell your son***, 'I do this because of what the LORD did for me when I came out of Egypt.' This observance will be for you like a sign on your hand and a reminder on your forehead that the law of the LORD is to be on your lips. For the LORD brought you out of Egypt with his mighty hand. You must keep this ordinance at the appointed time year after year.*
>
> **"In days to come, when your son asks you, 'What does this mean?' say to him, 'With a mighty hand the LORD brought us out of Egypt, out of the land of slavery.'"**
>
> —Exodus 13: 5–10, 14, emphasis added

Jesus did the same with the institution of the Lord's Supper. "Do this in remembrance of me," he said (Luke 22:19). He knew his "family" would need something to do regularly as a way to remember him, and he created what we call The Lord's Supper, or communion, to be sure we did.

So parents, let's get in the business of making memories—and repeating them day in and day out, year in and year out. Even if your own family was not this way, realize that this is a godly and good thing to do, with plenty of Bible precedent. Don't let stuffiness, laziness or cynicism rule the day in your house. Make up your own traditions. These moments can range from the profound to the goofy. The point is, your family needs them to help bind you all together and to have fun.

Why not make birthdays a chance not just to give gifts and have a party, but a time for everyone in the family to tell the birthday person just how special they are and how much we love them? We just get too busy—but these kinds of days and times actually help us to be unselfish and less preoccupied.

In our family, birthdays, Mother's Day and Father's Day were big, but Christmas, well, it was mega-huge. Nobody planned it that way, it just sort of happened over time. Getting the Christmas tree kicked off the season. We all headed out in the van and hit the neighborhood Christmas tree lot. After much deliberation we made our selection, then the kids and the family dog Riley had to run around and play hide and seek among the rest of the trees on the lot. Then we went home with our prize, and the boys and I set it up in the stand. Next, the whole family watched as I put on the lights. Then I got to relax and observe while Mom and the kids decorated the tree. And then, we capped it all off with an eggnog toast to celebrate and to mark the beginning of the Christmas season. To this day, our family holds those memories in a special, hallowed place of reverence in our hearts.

But that's our story. You need to go and write your own. So what are we waiting for? Let's get going and weave a fabric of memories that will bind our families together for a lifetime!

Group Discussion Questions

- Speaking of fabric, last week's homework challenged us as married couples to pray together every day for our families. How did you do? Share how praying together helped you this past week.

- What is the importance of having a family schedule? How does it help your family be closer? Can you give some examples that will encourage the group?

- What are some of the most helpful things your family does on a daily or weekly basis—things that help you build a closer family?

- Share with us some of your most fun, sacred and bonding family traditions. How did they come to be?

- How are you doing on family dinners and on Family Fabric in general? Rate your family on a scale of 1-10, with 10 being great. Are there some particular challenges for your family that you would like to share? Also share some of the changes you have decided to make to create a stronger, more healthy Family Fabric.

Notes:

My Daily Steps to a Stronger Family

Principle 2: **Family Fabric**

*Acknowledge and **take to heart this day** that the LORD is God in heaven above and on the earth below. There is no other. Keep his decrees and commands, which I am giving you today, so that it may go well with you and your children after you and that you may live long in the land the LORD your God gives you for all time.*

—Deuteronomy 4:39–40, emphasis added

Day One (day) _____ (date) _____:

Read Principle 2: **Family Fabric** Study and Group Discussion Guide.

- Spend a few minutes thinking about this principle and especially the scriptures in the Study Guide. How do you feel about the concept of "fabric"?

- Rate your family—do you have some traditions and memories that have helped you feel a sense of closeness and identity as a family? Is this something that is new or uncomfortable for you?

- What are some of the ways in which you feel your family is doing well in building family fabric?

_____

_____

_____

- Where can you do better?

_____

_____

_____

Day Two (day) _____ (date) _____:

Read Esther 9:26–28 and 1 Corinthians 11:23–26.

- Memories are powerful! They can make us happy, sad or angry.

- Take a few minutes today to think back to some of your own special memories from childhood.

- Some of you have many happy and special memories from your childhood, others of you do not. But you can create your own special memories and traditions in the family you are now raising.

- What are some traditions or habits you would like to create or strengthen in your own family?

Three traditions or habits I would like to create or strengthen in our family:

1. _____
2. _____
3. _____

Sometime today, take the time to share with your spouse your ideas and to hear theirs as well. Talk over how you can build them into your family life and help the fabric of your family to be stronger. Ask the kids for their ideas too.

Day Three (day) _____ (date) _____:

Read the section "Create Habits and Rhythms" in Principle 2.
Read Luke 2:41–42, 4:16, 9:23.

- What are some of the routines we need to establish in our homes just to make life run more efficiently and smoothly?

_____

_____

_____

- In what areas is your family doing well?

_____

_____

_____

- Where can you improve?

  _____

  _____

  _____

- Sometime today share with your spouse your ideas in this area. Hear what their ideas are and talk about how you can work together to improve your family routine.

Day Four (day) _____ (date) _____:

Reread the section "Use Mealtimes" in Principle 2.
Read Ecclesiastes 9:7–9; Luke 10:38–41; Acts 2:42–47.

These scriptures and many others talk about the importance of the simple act of sharing a meal together.

- Do you have a regular dinnertime as a family?
- Is the whole family there, and are you using the opportunity to talk and get closer as a family?
- What can you do to make it a more meaningful and enjoyable part of your family life?
- Is it a stressful time? What can you and your spouse do to work together to make it more fun and to get the kids more involved in helping out?

Three ideas to make the dinner hour more enjoyable and bonding for our family:

1. _____
2. _____
3. _____

Share these ideas with your spouse sometime today and talk about how you can work together to make dinner a great experience for your family.

Day Five (day) _____ (date) _____:
Reread the section "Celebrate Birthdays and Holidays" in Principle 2.
Read Exodus 13:5–10, 14.

- What are the special days and times of the year that mean the most
  to your family?

  _____

  _____

  _____

- What are you already doing to make things special, and what can
  you do to make them even more meaningful or memorable?

  _____

  _____

  _____

Discuss sometime today with your spouse what you can do to create special
holiday seasons, days and times for your family.

Day Six (day) _____ (date) _____:
Read 1 Corinthians 14:33a: "For God is not a God of disorder but of peace"; Luke
10:38–42.

- Special events and activities create closeness and connection for our
  families. However, these very things can also become stressful and
  burdensome. We have to be realistic about what we are actually
  able to do. Family traditions (and vacations) can take on a life of
  their own and become burdensome. Be realistic. How much can
  you handle? Are you trying to make things too perfect? Sometimes
  we have to step back and simplify. Family traditions don't have to be
  elaborate, expensive or time-consuming for the kids to be thrilled.
  Take an honest look—how do you handle the special times in your
  family's life? Do you get overwhelmed, upset? Do you help each
  other and support each other? Talk it over with your spouse. What
  can you do together to make these times more enjoyable and har-
  monious?

  _____

  _____

  _____

  _____

Day Seven (day) _____ (date) _____:

Read Principle 2 in its entirety.

- Now that you have had a week to think about this, write out your thoughts, convictions, dreams and ideas for a closer family fabric. Begin praying about these things consistently. Come prepared to discuss this chapter with the group.

  _____
  _____
  _____

- What are some of the memories you will want your children to have about your family when they begin families of their own?

  _____
  _____
  _____

Notes:

Principle 3: **Heart-to-Heart Talks**[1]

Give me your heart, my son,
And let your eyes delight in my ways.
> —Proverbs 23:26 (NASB)

Our families can be no closer than the degree to which we open our hearts and minds to one another. If we have a close family, it is because all of us express what we really think and feel—what is deepest on the inside. Closeness and love thrive when we really know each other on a heart-to-heart level. And to reach that goal, we are going to have to learn to talk heart to heart. Especially as our children mature, this becomes more and more important in being close to each other and to their parents.

It all starts with the relationship of parents to the kids. Talking heart to heart means we are operating on the principle of molding our children's hearts, not just controlling their actions.

Families (and individual family members) seem to go to extremes here—we clam up and don't really say what we think, or we feel free to speak to each other without any sort of godly restraint. With all the different kinds of personalities in our homes, it is no wonder that communication issues can become a major problem.

In the following passage the apostle Paul addresses the issue of how to build another kind of family—the church. Let's listen, learn and apply as we build our own families:

---

1. Some of the material in this chapter is taken from Sam and Geri Laing, *Raising Awesome Kids in Troubled Times—Reloaded* (Illumination Publishers, Spring, Texas: 2017).

Instead, speaking the truth in love, we will in all things grow up into him who is the Head, that is Christ. From him the whole body, joined and held together by every supporting ligament, grows and builds itself up in love, as each part does its work.

—Ephesians 4:15–16

There are two crucial lessons here. First, we have to *speak the truth* to each other. We can't build a close family if people are jammed up inside, holding back what they think, believe and feel. Families that do not share with each other what is really on their minds simply cannot be close. Clamming up may seem to preserve the peace, but it actually only serves to create distance and frustration.

But we also have to speak the truth *in love*. We can't just cut loose and say whatever comes to mind, regardless of how it may hurt or harm other family members.

So, parents, what do we need to do? *We need to encourage openness, yet godliness, in family communications.*

Let's consider some practical ways to help this happen.

- **Find quiet places and quiet moments to talk.** Raising kids and building a family can be a chaotic affair. We need to be intentional if we are to find time to speak with our kids in a relaxed, peaceful setting. Consider what Jesus said to his disciples in the midst of a particularly busy time: "Come with me by yourselves to a quiet place and get some rest" (Mark 6:31). Quiet times and talks with your children usually won't just happen—you will have to make them happen. In those moments, kids will open up and tell you what is going in their lives, hearts, minds and relationships.

- **Be careful to "be there" and not be distracted.** Most of us carry more anxiety and stress than we realize. We have to detach ourselves from the events of our day and focus on our families, or real communication just won't happen. This is where moms and dads can help each other by helping with the workload at home and by giving gentle reminders if we see our spouse getting too stressed and distracted—just as during family dinners my loving wife would sometimes lean over to me, her harried husband, and kindly whisper: "You're not here!"

- Don't speak or react too quickly. Kids do and say a lot that can provoke a quick response. If we are not careful, we will start talking before we get all the facts and/or understand their feelings. Let's heed this wise advice:

Everyone should be quick to listen, slow to speak and slow to become angry
—James 1:19

The purposes of a man's heart are deep waters,
but a man of understanding draws them out.
—Proverbs 20:5

To help your kids open up to you, try asking these questions:

- "And then what happened?"
- "And how did you feel about that?"
- "What do you think about …?"
- "Help me to understand about …."
- "Is there anything I have done to hurt your feelings?"

One last thought: Teach the kids how to speak to each other. When they are young, start with the basics of kindness and tone. As they mature, they will need to learn how to communicate with each other on a deeper level. Look at your family as a microcosm of the world. In order to build close friendships and live a happy adult life, your kids will have to learn how to deeply connect with others. The family is the best place to begin to learn how to do this.

One of the most important things you will ever do for your children is to help them learn to effectively communicate with their own brothers and sisters. Some of those relationships can be challenging. Coach them through those difficult relationships, even when it takes patience and work. Your kids will reap the benefit of being close to their siblings, and of learning how to build relationships with others as well.

Group Discussion Questions

- How has it been going praying with your family members this week? Do you need any help, advice or encouragement to get this going and keep it going?

- How do you rate your family communication?

- Discuss with the group your ratings of your family communications from the Daily Steps, Week Three, Day Two (pages 43–44).

- What can you do to help improve your family's communication? Do you need any ideas, encouragement or help?

Notes:

_____

_____

_____

_____

_____

_____

_____

_____

_____

_____

_____

_____

_____

_____

_____

_____

_____

_____

_____

_____

My Daily Steps to a Stronger Family

Principle 3: **Heart-to-Heart Talks**

*Acknowledge and **take to heart this day** that the LORD is God in heaven above and on the earth below. There is no other. Keep his decrees and commands, which I am giving you today, so that it may go well with you and your children after you and that you may live long in the land the LORD your God gives you for all time.*

—Deuteronomy 4:39–40, emphasis added

Day One (day) _____ (date) _____:

Read Principle 3: **Heart-to-Heart Talks** Study and Group Discussion Guide.

- What are your initial thoughts and reactions to this principle? How do you feel about your heart-to-heart communication with the kids?

- Are there some kids in your family that you have a more difficult time connecting with on a heart level?

- Begin praying daily that you will learn how to more effectively communicate, and that God will work in every situation to create a closer heart connection.

Day Two (day) _____ (date) _____:

Read Ephesians 4:15; 2 Corinthians 6:11–13: "We have spoken freely to you, Corinthians, and opened wide our hearts to you.... As a fair exchange—I speak as to my children—open wide your hearts also."

Let's figure out where we are, so we know where we need to go. Rate your and your spouse's level of heart-to-heart communication with each other:

Mom & Dad   ❑ Great   ❑ Very Good   ❑ Good   ❑ Fair   ❑ Needs Work

And with each family member:

Dad & _____ ❑ Great ❑ Very Good ❑ Good ❑ Fair ❑ Needs Work

Dad & _____ ❑ Great ❑ Very Good ❑ Good ❑ Fair ❑ Needs Work

Dad & _____ ❑ Great ❑ Very Good ❑ Good ❑ Fair ❑ Needs Work

Mom & _____ ❑ Great ❑ Very Good ❑ Good ❑ Fair ❑ Needs Work

Mom & _____ ❑ Great ❑ Very Good ❑ Good ❑ Fair ❑ Needs Work

Mom & _____ ❑ Great ❑ Very Good ❑ Good ❑ Fair ❑ Needs Work

Speaking from the heart is not easy for some of us. Perhaps it is difficult for you, your spouse or one or more of your children.

- Pray regularly about this.

- Make an effort to learn how to speak from the heart with your spouse and your children.

- Think of something you are worried about, sad about, happy about, or something you are learning. Share it with your spouse this week. If appropriate, share it with your children as well.

_____

_____

_____

Day Three (day) _____ (date) _____:

Read Ephesians 4:15–29; 2 Corinthians 6:12: "We are not withholding our affection from you."

- Today, pay attention to your words. Let your conversation with family members be positive, filled with heartfelt encouragement and affection.

- In every family, we will sometimes have to talk about difficult things. Even so, we must learn to do this in a warm, loving way. Ephesians 4:26–27 tells us "in your anger do not sin," but it also urges us not to "let the sun go down while you are still angry."

- Is there anyone you need to speak to about a hurt (including one you may have caused) or something you are angry or upset about? Pray about it and then share with them what is on your heart, *speaking the truth in love.*

Day Four (day) _____ (date) _____:

Reread Principle 3, the section on "practical ways to help this happen."
Read Luke 24:13–32.

Think about how Jesus communicated. It was after a long walk with him that his disciples observed, "Were not our hearts burning within us while he talked with us on the road and opened the Scriptures to us?" (Luke 24:32).

Quiet places and quiet moments
What would be times and places that would facilitate sharing from the heart with your family members? Think of what works best with each one of them, and write their name beside each suggestion.

- A walk outside _____

- A ride in the car _____

- Going out for breakfast, lunch, or ice cream _____

- At bedtime _____

- Other ideas: _____

  _____

  _____

- What will YOU do to make this happen?

  _____

  _____

  _____

Day Five (day) _____ (date) _____:

Review the five questions that help draw out others' feelings (see page 41).

- What do you learn about Jesus' sensitivity, perceptiveness and insight into people from the following passages?

- John 6:60–61

  _____

  _____

  _____

  _____

  _____

- John 11:32–36

  _____
  _____
  _____
  _____
  _____
  _____
  _____

- John 16:18–19

  _____
  _____
  _____
  _____
  _____
  _____
  _____

- John 19:25–27

  _____
  _____
  _____
  _____
  _____
  _____

- How does Jesus' example help you be a better heart-to-heart communicator in your family?

  _____
  _____
  _____
  _____
  _____
  _____

Day Six (day) _____ (date) _____:

Read James 1:19–20; Proverbs 18:13, 15; 20:5.

We can sometimes be unaware and a bit disconnected, missing things going on in the hearts and minds of our children and spouse. Or, we may over-react and speak too quickly, shutting others down and preventing genuine, heartfelt communication.

- How do you see yourself in this area?

- Ask your spouse for their candid evaluation. (Spouses, as you share with each other on this delicate matter, do so with love, sensitivity and humility.)

- How can you help each other become more effective communicators?

_____

_____

_____

- Pray about this individually and together.

Day Seven (day) _____ (date) _____:

Examine the following verses:

A gentle answer turns away wrath,
but a harsh word stirs up anger.
—Proverbs 15:1

He who guards his mouth and his tongue keeps himself from calamity.
—Proverbs 21:23

He who loves a pure heart and whose speech is gracious
will have the king for his friend.
—Proverbs 22:11

A word aptly spoken is like apples of gold in settings of silver.
—Proverbs 25: 11

Do not let any unwholesome talk come out of your mouths, but only what
is helpful for building others up according to their needs, that it may benefit

47

those who listen…. Be kind and compassionate to one another, forgiving each other, just as in Christ God forgave you.

—Ephesians 4:29, 32

- Pay attention today to the way your family speaks to one another—beginning with yourself. How are you speaking to your spouse, to your children? Also pay special attention to how your children are speaking to one another.

- At dinner tonight, or at your next family devotional, using the verses above, have a discussion about this topic with your family. Encourage everyone to make decisions to improve in how you speak to one another. Some apologies may be needed (even from Dad and Mom) and forgiveness extended. This is what strong, spiritual families do! We are not perfect, but we are willing to change and grow.

Notes:

_____

_____

_____

_____

_____

_____

_____

_____

_____

_____

_____

_____

_____

_____

Principle 4: **Resolve, Repair and Forgive**

His brothers...hated him and could not speak a kind word to him.
—Genesis 37:4

Pleasant words are a honeycomb,
sweet to the soul and healing to the bones.
—Proverbs 16:24

In this session we want to understand what kills and what builds communication in families. We also want to learn how to actually resolve problems, conflicts, hurts and anger among and between family members.

What are the blockages we need to recognize and remove?

Communication Killers[1]
1. Failure to listen (James 1:19)
2. Defensive listening (Proverbs 18:13)
3. Disrespect and dismissiveness (Proverbs 18:2)
4. Cutting, critical remarks (Ephesians 4:29)
5. Hinting (Ephesians 4:15)
6. Clamming up (Ephesians 4:26–27)
7. Blowing up (Proverbs 29:11)
8. Grumbling, griping and complaining (Philippians 2:14–15)
9. Lying (Proverbs 12:19)
10. Being distracted/distractions (Proverbs 8:6)

---

1. From *Friends and Lovers,* pp. 30–37.

What are the good habits we need to establish and maintain?

Communication Builders²

1. Daily dialogue (2 John 12)
2. Special times, special places (Mark 6:30–31)
3. Speaking heart to heart (2 Corinthians 6:11–13)
4. Learning the levels: facts, opinions and emotions (Proverbs 20:5)
5. Living and loving a little lighter (Romans 12:21)
6. Tone, touch, expression and attention (Mark 1:41, 10:16, 21, Proverbs 16:24)
7. Common courtesy (1 Corinthians 13:4–7, Ephesians 4:29)
8. Copious compliments (Philippians 4:8, 1 Thessalonians 5:11)
9. Sharing the spiritual (Matthew 18:20)
10. Saying I'm sorry; faithfully forgiving (Colossians 3:13)

Resolving, Repairing and Forgiving

Read Philippians 2:1–4, 4:2–3.

Conflicts, hurt feelings and offenses happen in families! As we learn to humbly, quickly and effectively resolve problems, we will be closer.

Here are some suggestions for parents when your kids have cross words and disagreements (all the while realizing that the ages of the kids involved makes a great deal of difference in how we handle each case):

- **Don't attempt to referee and resolve each and every argument or conflict between your children.** Instead, teach them to deal with things between themselves. If they have a hard time doing so, try sending them off together to talk it out. If they can't make progress, then step in and mediate.

- **If there has been offense on the part of both kids, help each child to see what they did/said that was hurtful.** Insist that they take full responsibility for their part and deal with themselves first. Assist them in coming to heartfelt sorrow for anything they did or said that was unkind, selfish or hurtful. Teach them how to express sincere apology and to extend forgiveness.

- **If need be, help them to properly express and get out in the open what their sibling did to hurt or offend them.**

2. From *Friends and Lovers*, pp. 38–47.

Teach them how to articulate those feelings and thoughts without going over the top in anger and emotion. (You may have to give time for the situation to cool down first.)

- **Help them to fully resolve the issue.** If we leave simmering anger or unresolved hurt feelings between our kids, they will not be close. Keep working until everyone's heart is clear.

- **Deal consistently with any recurring conflicts that continue to surface between children.** Some kids simply have trouble getting along with each other, and dealing with this will take patient and firm work by parents over time. In our own family, some siblings naturally got along great, and some tended to clash. We had to help the frequently clashing kids to humbly resolve conflict time and time again. (Finally, they grew older and became Christians and had some help from the Holy Spirit!)

- **Do not allow ongoing rudeness, harshness, sarcasm and ugly tones of voice to become the norm in your household**. To be sure, every family will have to deal with these issues, but our homes do not have to be like the ones we see on TV sitcoms. If you as parents persistently maintain a vision of a loving and courteous family, the Spirit will strengthen you to get there!

- **Do not allow a difficult or contentious child to set the tone or control the demeanor of your family.** Some kids by the assertion of their will or their continual complaining can ruin any family gathering. As parents you need to firmly decide what atmosphere you want (a godly one!) and simply not allow a surly or complaining child to sour it. Our suggestion: Send a sullen or out-of-control child to their room until they can come out and act properly. Don't back down or settle for half measures—this is a battle of wills parents can and must win. And, while the complainer is in their room working on their attitude, the rest of the family needs to go on with life and have a great time!

Group Discussion Questions

- Share with the group your areas of strength—what Communication Builders are your personal strong points? What are your spouse's strengths? Your family's strengths?

- What Communication Killers are you working to overcome? What does your spouse need to work on? Your family?

- How would you rate the atmosphere of your home? On a scale from 1 to 10, with 1 being poor and 10 being great, rate the level of warmth, encouragement and love in your family communication.

- Is there a difficult relationship between any of the children or any one of the kids and a parent that you need help with?

- Are there any difficult or thorny issues where you as parents tend to disagree on how to train, teach or correct the kids?

- What can we, as a group, pray about to help your family to communicate better?

Notes:

My Daily Steps to a Stronger Family

Principle 4: **Resolve, Repair and Forgive**

*Acknowledge and **take to heart this day** that the LORD is God in heaven above and on the earth below. There is no other. Keep his decrees and commands, which I am giving you today, so that it may go well with you and your children after you and that you may live long in the land the LORD your God gives you for all time.*

—Deuteronomy 4:39–40, emphasis added

Day One (day) _____ (date) _____:

Read Principle 4: **Resolve, Repair and Forgive** Study and Group Discussion Guide.

Let's first consider the latter section on "Resolving, Repairing and Forgiving":

- What are your initial thoughts and reactions?

  _____

  _____

- Do you believe that it is indeed possible for your family to be respectful and to learn how to resolve conflict?

  _____

  _____

- Do you see this as a biblical principle, or an impossible ideal?

  _____

- What can you do to increase your faith that your family can grow in this area?

  _____

  _____

Day Two (day) _____ (date) _____:

Read through Communication Killers 1–5 and the accompanying scriptures.

- Do you see yourself in any of these?
- Do you see any of them in your family dynamic?

Day Three (day) _____ (date) _____:

Read through Communication Killers 6–10 and the accompanying scriptures.

- Do you see yourself in any of these?
- Do you see any of them in your family dynamic?
- Share your observations from yesterday and today with your spouse.

Day Four (day) _____ (date) _____:

Read Communication Builders 1–5 and the accompanying scriptures.

- Do you see any of these as strengths in your own communication?
- In your spouse's?
- In your children's?
- Encourage each other with the things you do see in one another.

Day Five (day) _____ (date) _____:

Read through Communication Builders 6–10 and the accompanying scriptures.

- Do you see some of these as personal strengths?
- In your spouse?
- How about in the rest of the family?
- How can you begin to build these things in a greater way into your family interactions with one another? Would a family devotional (or several!) help?
- Pray about the things you are learning in this area.

Day Six (day) _____ (date) _____:

Read Philippians 2:1–4, 4: 2–3. Reread the section on "Resolving, Repairing and Forgiving."

- Which of these suggestions particularly speaks to you and your family?

- Talk to your spouse about them. Are you in agreement?

- Make some decisions together on what it will take for you, as a family, to build stronger, better communication.

Day Seven (day) _____ (date) _____:

Go over the decisions you made individually and as a couple.

- Talk about these things as a family.

- Pray about them individually, as a couple and as a family.

- Resolve to pray and ask God to help you make the changes and to build positive communication habits into your family life.

- Talk as a family about ways you can help each other. As you talk, remember to be positive, humble and kind.

Notes:

_____

_____

_____

_____

_____

_____

_____

_____

_____

_____

_____

_____

_____

_____

_____

_____

_____

_____

_____

_____

_____

_____

_____

_____

_____

_____

_____

Principle 5: **Godly Priorities, Sane Schedule**

"So do not worry, saying, 'What shall we eat?' or 'What shall we drink?' or 'What shall we wear?' For the pagans run after all these things, and your heavenly Father knows that you need them. But seek first his kingdom and his righteousness, and all these things will be given to you as well. Therefore do not worry about tomorrow, for tomorrow will worry about itself. Each day has enough trouble of its own."

—Matthew 6:31–34

Is it just me, or has life in the last few years gotten more intense and frenetic? Are we working harder and longer? Is technology taking over our schedules? Have homework, sports and after-school activities for kids gotten out of hand? Has somebody taken a few hours off the clock?

It is time to step back, take a deep breath, and take stock. It is time to take a hard look at our priorities and to get some sanity in our schedules.

Just what is the problem? Here are two likely culprits: conformity and competition.

Conformity

Jesus says in our theme passage above that we are not supposed to act like other people in the world—running here to there, anxious, breathless and mindless, in pursuit of worldly success. He makes a similar point in the passage below:

"My prayer is not that you take them out of the world but that you protect them

from the evil one. They are not of the world, even as I am not of it."
—John 17:15–16

The Bible teaches that we are to be transformed, not conformed:

> Do not **conform** *any longer to the pattern of this world, but be* **transformed** *by the renewing of your mind. Then you will be able to test and approve what God's will is—his good, pleasing and perfect will.*
> —Romans 12:2, emphasis added

But the temptation for God's people has always been to blend in and let the world shape us rather than the other way around. And one of the ways the world most affects us is in how we raise our kids. Unless we are watchful, we can just go along with what everyone around us is doing, giving no thought to spiritual principles and priorities.

And what happens to our families when we do that? Three things, all bad:

- We become anxiety-ridden.
- Our families become fragmented.
- We compromise our commitment to Jesus as Lord.

Competition

Our guilt buttons get pushed pretty hard if our kids don't measure up to others. We think we are a "bad parent" if our offspring are not superachievers perched at the top of whatever ladder we think they need to climb. So, we put them in every activity, every sport and every club under the sun. Let's face it, folks: When we do this, parenting has become wrongly focused. We are functioning from a desire to win a contest for worldly success rather than a passion to help our children come to know the Lord. We might even be pushing them to accomplish what we wished we had when we were growing up.

Where does all this show up?

Homework, Grades and Academics

Academics and learning are primarily an issue of character and discipline. The Scriptures declare that our focus needs to be on doing our work to the best of our ability, and for the glory of God:

> *Whatever you do, work at it with all your heart, as working for the Lord, not for men, since you know that you will receive an inheritance from the Lord as a reward. It is the Lord Christ you are serving.*
>   —Colossians 3:23–24

If we emphasize *effort* and *excellence*, we are teaching our kids the invaluable lesson of learning to do their best for God—and to leave the results to him.

Avoid doing homework *with* or *for* your kids. If we function that way, we are not helping them grow in self-discipline. Instead, teach them to go to their room or to a quiet place where they can work alone. If you put them at the kitchen table so you can continually monitor their progress, you are interfering with their learning how to discipline themselves. Hovering over them like a helicopter or sitting beside them like a watchdog does not help them grow up, and it will wear you out. Let them learn to work on their own.

What if they struggle in a subject? If this happens, we need to be concerned and try to figure out a solution, but that is a far cry from pressuring them to be at the top of the class and getting upset if they don't bring home perfect grades. You can step in and try to assess what the issue is, but be careful not to take the burden all upon yourself. What if your child brings home a bad grade? What I am about to say may sound like blasphemy, but an occasional bad grade can actually serve a good purpose—it tells a kid that he or she needs to put in more effort to learn the material. And, realize that your child's less-than-awesome grade might be well worth appreciating, if you know they have done the best they can!

What if your kid has a big test or tough assignment due on Monday or on the day after midweek service at church? Should you keep them home to study? Is it being legalistic to go to church and possibly let their grades suffer?

This may seem like a small matter, but in fact it is huge. Decisions like this are defining markers in our family life. They tell us what really matters most to us.

Our service to God, our worship and fellowship with the body of Christ, and our learning the Word are of greater priority than schoolwork. That is what *"seek first his kingdom"* means—*choosing a godly priority over a worldly one.* It is not that grades and schoolwork are not important; it is that they are not *most* important. Church comes first. Ask yourself this question: If you make these compromises now, while your kids are young, what message are you giving them about what should be most important to them later on in life? And let us say from years of observation: Kids who are raised with well-defined spiritual priorities have a far greater chance of one day becoming and remaining disciples of Christ than those who are not.

Sports

Kids' sports programs have mushroomed into a vast network of leagues, seasons and competitions. In years past, most organized sports took place at school, or kids played informally with others in their own neighborhood. Not so today. There are coaches to please; uniforms to buy; and practices, tournaments and parent meetings to attend. If you have more than one kid, life can get pretty hectic, running from one practice or game to the next. Aren't sports supposed to be fun? When did they become a hassle?

Let's step back and get some perspective. What is the purpose of children's sports, anyway?

- **Have fun.** Have we forgotten the obvious? Sports are fun! They are not just about winning and keeping score; sports are about the joy of play itself.

- **Make friends.** Sports are a great way for kids to make friends and for parents to get to know other families as well. The camaraderie and relationship with other players lasts far beyond the memories of who won and who lost.

- **Become a team player.** One of the greatest values of sport is in learning the give-and-take of being on a team. Kids see that some players are better than others but that every member of the team is important, and they all win or lose together.

- **Learn how to deal with winning and losing.** Your kids will experience victory and defeat in sports, and they need to learn how to cope graciously with both. To win and not gloat; to lose and not sulk—how many adults could stand to learn those lessons?

- **Grow in skill.** Life is about learning. Some things come easily, some take work. If our kids grasp how to get the most out of their talents and be the best they can be in a given sport, they are taking away something worthwhile from their participation.

Sanity in Our Schedules

Homework, sports, school clubs…it can become overwhelming. If you have more than one child, it can get downright brutal. Remember: We have to decide our priorities, and not just go along with what everyone around us is doing. And our priorities need to be shaped by Scripture.

Let us suggest some down-to-earth guidelines to help you keep a sane schedule.

- **Each child plays only one sport at a time.** With the mushrooming numbers of leagues and overlapping schedules, we have to make choices. One sport at a time! (The same is true for major extracurricular activities like school plays, etc.)

- **Take on only what your family can handle.** Some people can handle more than others and still maintain their emotional and spiritual life. Only do what you can do, not what some other family can do.

- **Sporting events and practices take second place to church activities.** Have your mind fully made up that worshipping God, learning the Bible and building relationships with spiritual people are more important than participation in sports. Tell the kids and the coach the way it will be before you sign up. Put God first! Families who compromise live to regret it.

- **Set realistic expectations for parents' attendance at practices and games.** Who says you have to be at every single one? Join with other team members' parents and agree to trade off on rides and attendance—you will be glad you did.

Let's put academics and sports in their proper place. They are not the be-all and end-all of life. So what if our kids don't grow up to go to the elite school or star as winning athletes? In five, ten, or twenty years, what will matter?

Faith Is the Victory

Jesus asked the disciples a penetrating question, one that will help us realize just what is at the center of this issue:

> *"If that is how God clothes the grass of the field, which is here today and tomorrow is thrown into the fire, will he not much more clothe you, O you of little faith?"*
>
> —Matthew 6:30

Isn't Jesus saying that at the heart of setting priorities and keeping a sane schedule is the issue of *faith*? Do we trust that God's way is best for our families? Do we believe he loves us enough to guide us into a fulfilled and happy life? Do we believe he is willing and able to give us "all these things" if we put him first? Isn't it about time we did?

Group Discussion Questions

- How would you characterize the intensity level of your family schedule? How much stress do you feel? Are there any pressure points where you need to step back and recalibrate?

- Share some experiences when you and your family acted in faith, put your priorities in the right place, and God honored his promise to give "all these things."

- How are the kids doing in school? Any worries there? Share any helpful advice, and feel free to ask for input on any difficult matters.

- What sports are your kids in at this time? How is it going? Has it been a positive experience in your family life? Is there an area of sports that is particularly challenging for your family or any family member?

- Do you communicate well as a couple about your schedules? About the kids' schedules? Are there any areas of scheduling and priorities you would like to discuss tonight?

- How is your faith holding up? Are you trusting God in the decisions you are making?

Notes:

My Daily Steps to a Stronger Family

Principle 5: **Godly Priorities, Sane Schedule**

*Acknowledge and **take to heart this day** that the LORD is God in heaven above and on the earth below. There is no other. Keep his decrees and commands, which I am giving you today, so that it may go well with you and your children after you and that you may live long in the land the LORD your God gives you for all time.*

—Deuteronomy 4:39–40, emphasis added

Day One (day) _____ (date) _____:

Read Principle 5: **Godly Priorities, Sane Schedule** Study and Group Discussion Guide.

- Take this opportunity to "step back, take a deep breath, and take stock" as you look at your family's schedule and priorities.

- Write down your initial thoughts and reactions. Are you feeling generally good about the pace of life in your family? Do you feel relaxed, or is there continual time pressure? Start praying for God to reveal to you any pressure points that need evaluation.

_____

_____

_____

Day Two (day) _____ (date) _____:

Reread the section in Principle 5 entitled "Conformity."
Read and meditate on John 17:15–16 and Romans 12:2.

- What are some of the pulls of the world that you experience in your own life individually, and as a family?

Sometimes we don't even realize that we have bought into and begun following the ways of the world. Romans 12:2 teaches that as our minds are renewed, we will be able to test and approve what God's will is. We can see through the world's lies and see more clearly God's will for our lives.

- What does that mean to you personally? How can you better understand what God's will is for your life and for your family's life?
- Do you need to develop the habit of a deeper study of the Bible?
- Do you need to talk more and work together better as husband and wife?
- Do you get help and input from other spiritual couples?

Day Three (day) _____ (date) _____:
Reread the section in Principle 5 entitled "Competition."
Read and reflect on Matthew 20:20–28.

- How does your own pride and competitiveness affect you as a parent and affect your family?
- Do you find yourself feeling guilty as a parent? Sometimes guilt is legitimate conviction from God and the Spirit, pointing us to changes that need to be made. At other times guilt is from Satan, the "accuser" (Revelation 12:10), appealing to our insecurities and pride.
- How does guilt affect you as a parent? How can you know when it is valid and when not?

_____

_____

_____

Day Four (day) _____ (date) _____:
Reread the section in Principle 5 entitled "Homework, Grades and Academics."
Read and carefully consider Colossians 3:23–24.

- How does the biblical principle of working with all our hearts, as working for the Lord, change our attitudes toward schoolwork and grades?

- Do you think your kids are learning the heart of working hard and giving their best?

- How are your kids doing in school? How is their schoolwork affecting your family life? Your church priorities?

- Are there any changes you need to make as parents and/or as a family in this area of life? Any change in perspective? Any change in action?

  _____

  _____

  _____

- Talk to each other and to some other spiritual couples this week about what you are learning and the commitments you are making.

Day Five (day) _____ (date) _____:

Reread the section in Principle 5 entitled "Sports."
Read and reflect on 1 Timothy 4:8.

- Are your children involved in sports at this time? Do you think you have had a godly attitude toward their involvement? How are you doing as a parent in helping your child develop healthy, godly attitudes about sports?

- What is the best thing about their involvement in sports?

- What is the greatest challenge in this area—for you, your child and your family?

  _____

  _____

  _____

Day Six (day) _____ (date) _____:

Reread the section in Principle 5 entitled "Sanity in Our Schedules."
Read and reflect on Matthew 6:31–34; Ephesians 4:15–16.

- What are the greatest challenges and stresses in your personal and family schedules?

- Talk to your spouse about this. Are you in agreement about the priorities and schedule you and your family should have?

- What are some decisions you can make together to put sanity and harmony into your family life?

_____

_____

_____

Day Seven (day) _____ (date) _____:

Reread the section in Principle 5 entitled "Faith Is the Victory."
Read and reflect on Matthew 6:26–30.

God reminds us to look at the way he takes care of the birds of the air and the flowers of the field—and he loves us more than them!

- Think back to some times in the past when you stepped out in faith and God blessed you.

_____

_____

_____

- What are some steps of faith you need to make now—for yourself and for your family?

_____

_____

_____

_____

_____

Notes:

_____

_____

_____

_____

_____

_____

_____

_____

_____

_____

_____

_____

_____

_____

_____

_____

_____

_____

_____

_____

_____

_____

_____

_____

_____

_____

_____

_____

_____

_____

Principle 6: **Church Connection**

*Although I hope to come to you soon, I am writing you these instructions so that,
if I am delayed, you will know how people ought to conduct themselves in God's
household, which is the church of the living God, the pillar and foundation of
the truth.*

—1 Timothy 3:14–15

How does the church fit in with building a strong family? What place does
God intend it to have in our family life?

The Place of the Church

To understand the place of the church in God's scheme of things, let's take
a look at some of the names he gives his church:

- **The body of Christ:** "Now I rejoice in what was suffered for you,
  and I fill up in my flesh what is still lacking in regard to Christ's afflic-
  tions, for the sake of his body, which is the church" (Colossians 1:24).

- **The temple of the living God:** "What agreement is there between the temple of God and idols? For we are the temple of the
  living God. As God has said: 'I will live with them and walk among
  them, and I will be their God, and they will be my people'" (2 Corinthians 6:16).

- **A chosen people, a royal priesthood, a holy nation, the
  people of God:** "But you are a chosen people, a royal priesthood,
  a holy nation, a people belonging to God, that you may declare the
  praises of him who called you out of darkness into his wonderful
  light. Once you were not a people, but now you are the people of

God" (1 Peter 2:9–10).

- **God's household:** "Consequently, you are no longer foreigners and aliens, but fellow citizens with God's people and members of God's household" (Ephesians 2:19).

- **The bride of Christ:** "Let us rejoice and be glad and give him glory! For the wedding of the Lamb has come, and his bride has made herself ready" (Revelation 19:7; see also Revelation 21:2, 9; 22:17).

The list above is quite impressive, and it is far from complete! Sometimes we look at the church in a worldly way, through human eyes alone: "I want my family to be close to *God*, but the church, well, that's just…*people*." How wrong we are to think that way, and how it must grieve God when we do! No, the church is God's creation, planned for his glory and for our blessing and benefit. Let us value the church as highly as God does and give her the respect and reverence she deserves. And let us teach our families to do the same. Kids who are raised with a high view of the church are far more likely to end up giving their lives to Jesus as they mature.

The Purpose of the Church

The church is highly valued by God, but exactly what is its purpose? What role is it meant to play in our lives, and in particular, in our family's life?

God gives us the church to help us grow to become like Jesus.

> *Then we will no longer be infants, tossed back and forth by the waves, and blown here and there by every wind of teaching and by the cunning and craftiness of men in their deceitful scheming. Instead, speaking the truth in love, we will in all things grow up into him who is the Head, that is, Christ. From him the whole body, joined and held together by every supporting ligament, grows and builds itself up in love, as each part does its work.*
> —Ephesians 4:14–16

As we are effectively involved in the church, we grow individually and as a family. With the church, we mature; without the church, we remain selfish and undeveloped. God will use the church—its teaching, example and influence—to teach us how to build a close, loving and spiritual family.

God uses the church to equip us to effectively serve him.

It was he who gave some to be apostles, some to be prophets, some to be evangelists, and some to be pastors and teachers, to prepare God's people for works of service, so that the body of Christ may be built up until we all reach unity in the faith and in the knowledge of the Son of God and become mature, attaining to the whole measure of the fullness of Christ.

—Ephesians 4:11–13

The church is the place where you and your family will be enabled and empowered to serve God and others. The church is God's talent-search organism! It is here where your family members' talents will be discovered and developed (see Romans 12:3–8).

The Promise of the Church

I pray that out of his glorious riches he may strengthen you with power through his Spirit in your inner being, so that Christ may dwell in your hearts through faith. And I pray that you, being rooted and established in love, may have power, **together with all the saints,** *to grasp how wide and long and high and deep is the love of Christ, and to know this love that surpasses knowledge—that you may be filled to the measure of all the fullness of God.*

Now to him who is able to do immeasurably more than all we ask or imagine, according to his power that is at work within us, to him be glory in the church and in Christ Jesus throughout all generations, for ever and ever! Amen.

—Ephesians 3:16–21, emphasis added

Notice in this passage that we experience the power of God "together with all the saints." We cannot isolate or distance our families from the community of the saints and expect it to be strong! The church is God's way of helping us be empowered and led by the Holy Spirit. Households devoted to the church benefit from the teaching, discipling and influence of godly leaders (Ephesians 4:11–13). The church teaches us to study the Word, to pray together, to solve problems, to forgive and to express love.

The Priority of the Church

Seeing God's plan and promise, is it any wonder that he wants us to make the church one of our family's top priorities? Our participation, investment in and commitment to the church must be deep, intense and unshakable.

Consider these verses:

Let us hold unswervingly to the hope we profess, for he who promised is faithful. And let us consider how we may spur one another on toward love and good deeds. Let us not give up meeting together, as some are in the habit of doing, but let us encourage one another—and all the more as you see the Day approaching.

—Hebrews 10:23–25

The body is a unit, though it is made up of many parts; and though all its parts are many, they form one body....

Now the body is not made up of one part but of many. If the foot should say, "Because I am not a hand, I do not belong to the body," it would not for that reason cease to be part of the body. And if the ear should say, "Because I am not an eye, I do not belong to the body," it would not for that reason cease to be part of the body....

But in fact God has arranged the parts in the body, every one of them, just as he wanted them to be....

The eye cannot say to the hand, "I don't need you!" And the head cannot say to the feet, "I don't need you!"... There should be no division in the body, but...its parts should have equal concern for each other. If one part suffers, every part suffers with it; if one part is honored, every part rejoices with it.

Now you are the body of Christ, and each one of you is a part of it.

—1 Corinthians 12:12, 14–16, 18, 21, 24–27

Our family needs the church! The church needs our family! We cannot, must not, let our family become marginal participants. "Church" is not just something we *do*—it is who we *are*. Never should we speak of the church as "they." Far from it—the church is "we"!

The Problem of the Church

Church problems? Haven't we been saying that the church is a taste of heaven on earth?

I have a friend in the ministry who says, "My church would be doing great if it weren't for the people in it." How true! The church is indeed a taste of heaven, but until we actually arrive there, we are still a work in progress and will have our problems.

What are some of the problems families can have in the church?

- **Leaders may fail us and fail our children.** While the Bible makes it clear that the church needs leaders, it also informs us that leaders sometimes falter. It is not leaders themselves, but the God they teach us about to whom we owe our deepest allegiance and in whom we place our ultimate faith. A couple of the leaders who were mentoring my teenage sons fell from the faith. We used those painful moments as opportunities to teach our boys that although people may fail, God never does. We also taught them that although leaders were and are fallible, they still needed leadership and to respect whomever God placed in their ministry at any particular time.

- **There may be worldliness in the youth ministry.** Not all kids being raised in church families are going to end up following Jesus. Some will turn out great; some may be drawn to the world. We do not need to lose heart or lose trust when this happens. Show your kids that these kinds of problems occurred in the early church and were addressed in the Word. As you talk about these issues, take care not to come off as self-righteous or critical of the church, but simply as being honest and truthful. This will help our children to deal with these issues without losing faith in God and his people.

- **Your kids may feel left out; there may be cliquishness in the youth ministry.** One of the most pervasive issues young people have to deal with out in the world is cliquishness in their peer groups. Regrettably, those attitudes may make their way into the kids in our churches. It is a problem every youth ministry will need to address at some time. If your kids feel left out or are having a hard time feeling close to others, be careful not to overreact, prejudge or write off the whole ministry. Become a part of the solution. Take the time to talk to the leaders and find out what is going on.

- **There will be conflicts and hurt feelings between our kids and other kids in the church.** Have you ever noticed that Jesus had to spend quite a bit of time correcting the behaviors and attitudes of his twelve apostles toward one another? They argued about who was the greatest; they were selfish and competitive. How about the letters to the churches? Many of them were written to solve problems having to do with conflicts and hurt feelings among Christians. Remember this: The church is unique not because it is devoid of conflict, but because God teaches and empowers the church to resolve conflicts in a loving and righteous manner.

Here are some principles and suggestions as your family lives its life in the church:

- **Your commitment to the church is not based on the church or leaders being perfect.** Jesus is perfect. All the rest of us have a ways to go. Maintain respect for the church and church leaders, even when you see weaknesses.

- **If your children have conflicts with other kids, be careful not to jump to conclusions, pull back or overreact.** Remember: It is hard to be objective when it comes to our own kids. Let this scripture be deeply in your heart: "The first to present his case seems right, till another comes forward and questions him" (Proverbs 18:17).

- **Deal with any conflicts involving your family in a godly manner.** Don't blow up or clam up. Don't start gossiping and complaining. Don't try to fix every problem for your kids—teach them how to talk things out with their peers. If you have a personal issue, go directly to the person or people involved, but do so with a gentle and humble spirit, recognizing that you too are human and a sinner. If you can't solve the problem on your own, call in wise, respected people to help you sort it out.

Prizing the Church

Make room for us in your hearts. We have wronged no one, we have corrupted no one, we have exploited no one. I do not say this to condemn you; I have said before that you have such a place in our hearts that we would live or die with you. I have great confidence in you; I take great pride in you. I am greatly encouraged; in all our troubles my joy knows no bounds.
—2 Corinthians 7:2–4

The church in Corinth was not easy for Paul to work with. They were an immature, worldly bunch. They had arguments and conflicts. They had a prideful spirit. There was sin in their midst. You would think Paul would have lost respect and trust for them. Not so! He confronted their sin. He dealt with them firmly—but he always maintained a respectful, hopeful attitude and believed the best of them.

Parents, keep a loving and respectful spirit about your church, and help your kids do the same. Make it your rule to never run down the church or the church leaders in front of your kids. If you have to deal with difficult matters, do so communicating a spirit of high esteem for your church. You will be doing your kids a great service.

Show proper respect to everyone: Love the brotherhood of believers, fear God, honor the king.

—1 Peter 2:17

To him be glory in the church and in Christ Jesus throughout all generations, for ever and ever! Amen.

—Ephesians 3:21

Group Discussion Questions

- What are some of the ways the church has been a blessing to your marriage and family? Where would you be today without the good influence of God's church upon your family?

- What are some of the reasons you love and respect the church?

- How has the church helped you and your kids grow? Helped you form good friendships? Helped you develop your talents, find ways to serve God, serve others and be useful?

- Have you ever had to work through conflicts and problems in the church? Share with the group how applying scriptural principles helped you.

- How do your kids feel about the church? Is there anything you need to do to help them get more involved?

- Have you ever had to go through a time when you saw difficulties and problems in the church? How did you see God demonstrate his love, faithfulness and power in that time? Are you glad you stayed faithful to God and the church through a season of testing and difficulty? What lessons did you learn?

Notes:

Week Six
My Daily Steps to a Stronger Family

Principle 6: **Church Connection**

*Acknowledge and **take to heart this day** that the LORD is God in heaven above and on the earth below. There is no other. Keep his decrees and commands, which I am giving you today, so that it may go well with you and your children after you and that you may live long in the land the LORD your God gives you for all time.*

—Deuteronomy 4:39–40, emphasis added

Day One (day) _____ (date) _____:

Read Principle 6: **Church Connection** Study and Group Discussion Guide. Review the first section, "The Place of the Church."

- What do the names that God gives the church tell you about his view of it?

- Is the church just another human society, or is there more to it? What makes the church different and vastly more important than other organizations?

- Do you think God views your local church and its ministry in the same elevated way as he describes the church in these verses?

- Would you say that your view and opinion of the church has been as high as God's?

- Why do you think it is important for you as a parent to have a high opinion of your church and to teach your children to do the same?

Day Two (day) _____ (date) _____:

Review and study the section in Principle 6 entitled "The Purpose of the Church." Read and reflect on Ephesians 4:11–16.

What are the two great purposes of the church as given in the Study Guide?

1. _____

2. _____

- How has the church helped you and your family to grow to be more like Christ?

- How has the church helped teach, equip and train your family? What can you do to maximize this particular blessing of the church's ministry for your family?

_____

_____

_____

Day Three (day) _____ (date) _____:

Review and study the section in Principle 6 entitled "The Promise of the Church." Study Ephesians 3:14–21.

- From this passage, what are some of God's promises to you and your family through the church?

_____

_____

_____

- Why is it true that *together with all the saints* we are strengthened with power, enabled to better grasp the love of Christ and filled with the fullness of God? Can we do that all on our own? Why not?

- List five ways God has used the church to bless your life and your family's life.

1. _____

2. _____

3. _____

4. _____

5. _____

For the rest of this week, thank God in prayer every day for these blessings.

Day Four (day) _____ (date) _____:

Review and study the section in Principle 6 entitled "The Priority of the Church."
Study Hebrews 10:23–25, 1 Corinthians 12:12–27.

- What do these scriptures tell you about the importance of your family's connection to the church? How directly is your family's spiritual vitality associated with your local congregation?

- Why should the church and its activities have a high priority in your family's schedule?

_____

_____

_____

- How tightly is your family spiritually, relationally and emotionally connected to your local church?

- What is your feeling about your local congregation? Do you feel close to it? To your family group? Do you regularly pray for your church and for its leaders?

- Are your kids involved in their part of the local ministry? Are you and your family making the effort to be involved and stay involved?

Day Five (day) _____ (date) _____:

Review and study the section in Principle 6 entitled "The Problem of the Church."
Read 1 Corinthians 1:1–12, 3:1–4, 6:1–6; 2 Corinthians 7:2–4.

There are four church problems listed in the Study Guide that can directly affect our family—briefly summarize what they are:

1. _____

2. _____

3. _____

4. _____

- If you have encountered any of these kinds of problems, have you allowed this to discourage you, hurt your faith or diminish your family's involvement in the church? How does God want you to respond?

- What can you do to overcome these kinds of issues? (See the principles and suggestions listed in this section of the Study Guide.) Is there any conflict or difficulty you need help with now? Do you need to seek advice and resolution in private conversation with appropriate church leaders?

_____

_____

_____

Day Six (day) _____ (date) _____:

Briefly review the section in Principle 6 entitled "The Problem of the Church." Read 1 Corinthians 1:1–12, 3:1–4, 6:1–6.

- What are some of the problems Paul identifies in the church at Corinth?

- How do they compare in intensity with issues in your congregation?

- What was Paul's attitude as he addressed these issues?

- What is Paul's predominant sentiment in 1 Corinthians 1:1–9? What does that tell you about what our attitude ought to be as we deal with the reality of life in our local church?

- In this same passage, Paul describes how he prays passionately for the church in Corinth (v. 4). How does prayer help the church and help our attitude? Resolve to pray for your church, its leaders, and any difficult people and situations. Always include your church in your family prayers, being thankful and faithful.

Day Seven (day) _____ (date) _____:

Review and study the section in Principle 6 entitled "Prizing the Church."

Read and reflect upon 1 Peter 2:17; Ephesians 3:21; 2 Corinthians 7:2–4.

List below five reasons you love and prize your local church:

1. _____

2. _____

3. _____

4. _____

5. _____

- Thank God for these things in prayer.

- Share these with your spouse and with your family at dinner to-night or at your next family devotional, and encourage everyone else to do the same.

Notes:

_____

_____

_____

_____

_____

_____

_____

_____

_____

_____

_____

_____

_____

_____

_____

_____

_____

_____

_____

_____

_____

_____

_____

_____

_____

_____

_____

_____

_____

_____

Principle 7: **Faith, Fun and Laughter**

A cheerful heart is good medicine, but a crushed spirit dries up the bones.

—Proverbs 17:22

He has made everything beautiful in its time. He has also set eternity in the hearts of men; yet they cannot fathom what God has done from beginning to end. I know that there is nothing better for men than to be happy and do good while they live. That everyone may eat and drink, and find satisfaction in all his toil—this is the gift of God.

—Ecclesiastes 3:11–13

Go, eat your food with gladness, and drink your wine with a joyful heart, for it is now that God favors what you do. Always be clothed in white, and always anoint your head with oil. Enjoy life with your wife, whom you love, all the days of this meaningless life that God has given you under the sun—all your mean- ingless days. For this is your lot in life and in your toilsome labor under the sun.

—Ecclesiastes 9:7–9

Rejoice in the Lord always. I will say it again: Rejoice! Let your gentleness be evident to all. The Lord is near. Do not be anxious about anything, but in everything, by prayer and petition, with thanksgiving, present your requests to God. And the peace of God, which transcends all understanding, will guard your hearts and your minds in Christ Jesus.

—Philippians 4:4–7

A Fun Atmosphere

So what is the atmosphere like at your house? What's the mood? *Upbeat? Fun? Expectant? Lighthearted? Adventurous? Lots of smiles, laughter and hugs?* If not, let's get to work on it.

84

One of the revolutionary concepts Jesus brought into the religious world was the notion that life with God could be *fun*:

> *But when the chief priests and the teachers of the law saw the wonderful things he did and the children shouting in the temple area, "Hosanna to the Son of David," they were indignant.*
> *Do you hear what these children are saying?" they asked him.*
> *"Yes," replied Jesus, "have you never read,*
> *"'From the lips of children and infants*
> *you have ordained praise'?"*
>
> —Matthew 21:15–16

What's going on here—kids shouting in the temple? Oh, no! God must be offended!

Take a look at Jesus' life. He broke the stuffy, man-made rules that had been encrusted onto the Faith. He went to weddings. He shared meals with others. He loved children. He spent time outside—sailing, walking, talking and being with people. He called God his Father and encouraged us to do the same.

The Power of Laughter

One of the worst things that can happen to a family is when we allow a negative, pessimistic, gloomy, worried and anxious spirit to take hold. If we want to have the fruits of the Holy Spirit in our life—and in our home life—we have to remember that the second one on the list, just behind love, is *joy* (see Galatians 5:22).

Laughter is like a tonic. It makes you healthier. Studies prove it.

Here is what laughter does:

- Decreases stress hormone levels
- Acts as a natural antidepressant
- Promotes muscle relaxation
- Strengthens the immune system
- Helps in pain reduction
- Lowers blood pressure
- Helps cardiovascular conditioning

Other studies tell us that kids laugh well over 200 times a day and that adults laugh about 15 times a day. So who do we need to be like—grumpy adults or happy kids?

> *At that time the disciples came to Jesus and asked, "Who is the greatest in the kingdom of heaven?" He called a little child and had him stand among them. And he said: "I tell you the truth, unless you change and become like little children, you will never enter the kingdom of heaven. Therefore, whoever humbles himself like this child is the greatest in the kingdom of heaven."*
>
> —Matthew 18:1–4

Parents, we have lots of work to do to raise our kids and build a family. There are meals to fix, clothes to wash and rooms to clean; there is homework to do…. There are behaviors to correct, problems to solve, tears to dry…and, oh yeah, besides all that, we have to make a living! Let's not wait to have fun until we get it all done or our kids are perfect. One day we will look back and long for these crazy days—let's appreciate them while they are here.

Let's not just raise our children—let's *enjoy* them. Have you taken the time lately to sit back and take delight in just how special each one is? Have you noticed and appreciated the quirky little things that make them who they are, that make them a delight?

You know what? If you *like* your children, if you *take delight* in them, raising them will be a lot easier. When they know that your home and family is the happiest place in their world, they will want to keep it that way. The happier your home, the more motivated your kids will be to please you—who would want to spoil all the fun?

Geri often shares about a prayer she used to pray in the midst of the chaos of raising four little ones: "God, I know you love and like these children. So do I, but right now I'm having a hard time. Help me to see what you see in them—show me something in them to like today!" At any stage of parenting, sometimes all we can see in our kids are the problems, stresses and challenges. We need to stop and appreciate the amazing gifts that our children are to us, even when they (and we!) may not be at our best.

A Faithful Atmosphere

Let's work on having a positive, faithful atmosphere in our homes. Almost without thinking, we can slip into a complaining spirit. We can focus on the dark side of life. We can make worrying the norm. Do you realize that it takes no more effort to think positively than negatively? But wait; let's re-think that—because in reality, worry and fretting are exhausting!

Christianity is all about Good News. In every situation, we need to focus on the Good News that God brings to it. In our conversations, our sharing at family meals, our attitudes toward whatever is going on, let's keep looking for and focusing on the Good News.

The Bible tells us we should overflow with hope:

> *May the God of hope fill you with all joy and peace as you trust in him, so that you may overflow with hope by the power of the Holy Spirit.*
> —Romans 15:13

Let's look at everything that happens in the life of our family and see that God can—and will—bring good out of it (Romans 8:28). Parents, your faith sets the tone. When the kids have a tough day at school, when they come home with a bad report card, when they have a problem with a friend—let's always remind everyone to look for what God can do to turn it around for the good.

We don't want worldliness to take root in our homes. When we think of "worldliness" we usually equate it with sins like greed, lust and anger. But worldly thinking is not limited to those kinds of things. Worldliness is also a faithless, pessimistic spirit. Just as much as we don't want those "big" sins to take root in our homes, we should work to keep out worldly worrying and anxiety.

In most marriages, one of us tends to be the worrier, and one of us is more positive. Let's not shut down the positive partner. Let's allow their faith and smile to flourish in our family! Don't quench their spirit or The Spirit! And if you have a kid who tends to be a worrier, don't let him or her set the tone, either.

We can decide: *Our family is going to be full of faith. Our family is going to be happy.* Our home is going to be a joyful place. We get what we decide. We get what we expect.

87

Learn to Lighten Up

> *Do not be overrighteous,*
> *neither be overwise—*
> *why destroy yourself?*
> *Do not be overwicked,*
> *and do not be a fool—*
> *why die before your time?*
> *It is good to grasp the one*
> *and not let go of the other.*
> *The man who fears God will avoid all extremes.*
>
> —Ecclesiastes 7:16–18

Respect, obedience and discipline—we know how important they are in raising kids. But it is also good to know when to loosen the reins and not be so rigid.

When Alexandra was little, she constantly spilled her milk and made a mess at the dinner table. She wasn't trying to be that way; she just was (and still is) so exuberant that she kind of forgot what she was doing. One night, Geri became frustrated with Alexandra's continued clumsiness: "If you spill your milk one more time, you're going to get a spanking you'll never forget!" she said. Sure enough, just a few minutes later, it happened again. Alexandra burst out crying—The Spanking of a Lifetime was coming. Geri looked over at me for help, knowing that she had overreacted earlier. I looked back at her and just shrugged my shoulders, knowing we were in a predicament.

As she headed up the stairs with Alexandra, Geri had to think fast. She got a brilliant idea. They went into Alexandra's room, and Geri had her bend over. But instead of administering the expected fearsome discipline, Geri just quickly tapped her gently three times on the backside. Alexandra looked around in shock, wondering what was going on. "I told you this would be a spanking you would never forget," Geri said. When they came back down, we all cracked up laughing—and to this very day, we remember the fabled Spanking of a Lifetime!

Group Discussion Questions

- How is the mood in your home? Would you say that it is characterized by a joyful, carefree spirit? Are you laughing together?

✳ • What can you do to build a faithful, positive, Good News attitude in your home?

• Does your family have an unofficial Social Chairman—a fun and games person? Who in your family are the most happy, fun people? Are you letting them influence the home atmosphere?

✳ • What are some things your family does to have fun? Share them with the group. Are you doing those things very often? How can you as a family do more fun things?

Notes:

My Daily Steps to a Stronger Family

Principle 7: **Faith, Fun and Laughter**

Acknowledge and **take to heart this day** *that the* LORD *is God in heaven above and on the earth below. There is no other. Keep his decrees and commands, which I am giving you today, so that it may go well with you and your children after you and that you may live long in the land the* LORD *your God gives you for all time.*

—Deuteronomy 4:39–40, emphasis added

Day One (day) _____ (date) _____:

Read Principle 7: **Faith, Fun and Laughter** Study and Group Discussion Guide. Then review the first section, "A Fun Atmosphere."
Read and reflect on Proverbs 17:22; Ecclesiastes 3:11–13, 9:7–9; Matthew 21:15–16.

- What do you think the atmosphere was like around Jesus?
- What is the atmosphere in your home like? Is it characterized more by fun and laughter or by seriousness, heaviness and sadness?

Day Two (day) _____ (date) _____:

Read in Principle 7 the section "The Power of Laughter."
Read and reflect on Matthew 18:1–4.

- How does laughter help ease the burdens of life? How does it help your family be closer? How does it help the kids? How does it help you?
- Studies show kids laugh over 200 times a day and that grown-ups

laugh about 15 times a day. How do you think Matthew 18:1–4 applies here?

- Has your family been laughing enough? Can we decide to laugh more in our family? Try laughing more and see what the results are in terms of obedience, cooperativeness and peace in your home.

- Plan a "joke night" at dinner this week. Tell funny stories from your own childhood. Talk about the funniest scenes in movies your family loves. Recall some hilarious moments during church services. Get the laughter going!

Day Three (day) _____ (date) _____:

Review in Principle 7 the section entitled "The Power of Laughter."
Read Psalm 139:13–16.

- Make a list of the special, unique, quirky and fun things about each of your kids and your spouse. Thank God for these things in prayer.

- Share your list with the family at dinner. Get everyone else in the family to share their thoughts as well. As people share, remember: You are not making fun of each other—these are things you delight in and that make your family members special!

Day Four (day) _____ (date) _____:

Read in Principle 7 the section entitled "A Faithful Atmosphere."
Read and reflect on Romans 8:28–39, 15:13.

These scriptures teach us that God is working out everything for our good and that he can take even the bad things and turn them to our advantage.

- This week in family devotional time or at dinner, have the family share about some occasions when God turned a sad or difficult situation around. Start building a faithful, positive spirit in your home.

- Words are important! Set that example in your own faith and in the way you speak. Even in the little things that can go wrong or vex us in family life, let's keep a positive, faithful spirit. Let's nix the grumbling (see Philippians 2:14–15).

"Do everything w/o grumbling or arguing ... result → we may become blameless & pure 92 children of God w/o fault in a warped/corrupt generation — Then, you will shine!"

Day Five (day) _____ (date) _____:

Review in Principle 7 the section "A Faithful Atmosphere."
Read and reflect Numbers 6:24–26; Isaiah 43:3–4, 65:19, Luke 15:20–24.

- Do you believe that God delights in you? Do you sense the joy of his love for you? Do you feel his smile?
- Write down what you think God likes about you and delights in when he thinks about you. → *I Thess 2:8*
- Do your children feel that you delight in them? How can you better show them your delight? How can we enjoy our children and not just raise them?

Day Six (day) _____ (date) _____:

Review in Principle 7 the section "A Faithful Atmosphere."
Read and reflect on 1 Corinthians 15:51–57; 2 Corinthians 2:14; 1 John 5:3–5.

- We are victorious in Christ! He has won the battle! Build a victory spirit in your home. Over and over, say things like: *God is with us. This will all work out. God will meet all our needs. We are more than conquerors. We can do all things through Christ. We are victors, not victims.* Make these kinds of declarations a habit in your family conversation.

- Are you letting the positive, happy souls in your family shine, or do you tend to shut them down? Let the fun-loving, positive family members have the influence God intends them to have.

Day Seven (day) _____ (date) _____:

Review in Principle 7 the section "Learn to Lighten Up."
Read and reflect on Ecclesiastes 7:16–18; Matthew 11:28–30; Luke 15:22–25; Psalm 150.

Jesus said his yoke is easy and his burden is light. If life in our home is just one big pressure cooker, then we need to learn from Jesus how to lighten up and live differently.

- Plan a movie night in the next few days—a comedy. Put a blanket on the floor, share an easy meal, and have a good time laughing together.

- How about some music and dancing? Some of us have little or no rhythm, but who cares? Put on some fun music and cut loose!

- Come up with your own ideas for family fun and games—those are the best ones. These times don't have to be elaborate, complicated or expensive—they can even be kind of silly. And if you really want to have a blast—*let the kids get in on the planning!*

Notes:

_____

_____

_____

_____

_____

_____

_____

_____

_____

_____

_____

_____

_____

_____

_____

_____

_____

_____

_____

_____

_____

_____

_____

_____

_____

_____

_____

_____

Principle 8: **Family Spirituality**

Like newborn babies, crave pure spiritual milk, so that by it you may grow up in your salvation…. You also, like living stones, are being built into a spiritual house to be a holy priesthood, offering spiritual sacrifices acceptable to God through Jesus Christ.

—1 Peter 2:2, 5

We have not received the spirit of the world but the Spirit who is from God, that we may understand what God has freely given us. This is what we speak, not in words taught us by human wisdom but in words taught by the Spirit, expressing spiritual truths in spiritual words.

—1 Corinthians 2:12–13

What do we mean by the term "spirituality"?

Perhaps the best way to describe this concept is by saying that it means we are striving to be on the inside what we are trying to *do* on the outside. It means that, as Jesus said in the Sermon on the Mount, we do not seek to merely appear religious, but we instead function out of a deep, genuine walk with God.

"And when you pray, do not be like the hypocrites, for they love to pray standing in the synagogues and on the street corners to be seen by men. I tell you the truth, they have received their reward in full. But when you pray, go into your room, close the door and pray to your Father, who is unseen. Then your Father, who sees what is done in secret, will reward you."

—Matthew. 6:5–6

We will come back to prayer in a moment, but do you see the point Jesus is making? It is this: *Our spiritual life must originate from the inside, from our deepest heart, our deepest being.* Anything less is not pleasing to God.

Have you noticed how children react to insincerity? They seem to have innate radar that can spot phoniness or fakeness a mile away: "That's just pretend!" "That's not real!" Sure, they have a great capacity to imagine and can be naïve. But our kids can tell when Mom and Dad are the real deal, and they perceive what is most important to us. They know if we genuinely love God and walk with him or if we are just going through the motions.

This may be uncomfortable for us to think about and deal with, but folks, it may be the most essential of the Essential 8 Principles.

It is not that parents need to be perfect or that we can never make a mistake. If that is the standard, then we're all goners! No, we all fall short, we all sin, we all have our weaknesses—and our kids will see them, just as plain as day, because who we are at home is who we really are. What the kids need to see in us is not perfection—that role is for Jesus alone—what they need to see in us is *genuineness and sincerity*. And that is where spirituality comes in.

As parents we must be seeking to sincerely walk with God. Our personal prayer life, our personal Bible study, our efforts to live righteously—all of this goes into making us genuinely spiritual people. If our kids see that we consistently spend time in personal Bible study, that we are devoted to prayer, that we are seeking to grow to be like Christ and that we humbly acknowledge our shortcomings, they will know in their hearts that we are seeking to be the people we are teaching them to become.

How do we transmit spirituality into our family life?

Here are some basics:

Family Prayer

Our children will learn to pray by hearing us pray. They will learn to experience God's presence as they see that it is real through family prayer. We should pray with our children at regular times such as mealtimes and bedtime—not in a routine or rote manner, but from the heart. Pray with the kids as they leave for school, as you drive to church, as they face difficulties at school or with friends. Prayer needs to be the air we breathe. It needs to be something our family does easily, frequently and naturally. So:

*Do not be anxious about anything, but **in everything**, by prayer and petition, with thanksgiving, present your requests to God.*
—Philippians 4:6, emphasis added

*Be joyful always; **pray continually**; give thanks in all circumstances, for this is God's will for you in Christ Jesus.*
—1 Thessalonians 5:16–18, emphasis added

*And pray in the Spirit on **all occasions** with all kinds of prayers and requests. With this in mind, be alert and always keep on praying for all the saints.*
—Ephesians 6:18, emphasis added

Family Bible Study and Spiritual Conversation

Hear, O Israel: The LORD our God, the LORD is one. Love the LORD your God with all your heart and with all your soul and with all your strength. These commandments that I give you today are to be upon your hearts. Impress them on your children. Talk about them when you sit at home and when you walk along the road, when you lie down and when you get up. Tie them as symbols on your hands and bind them on your foreheads. Write them on the doorframes of your houses and on your gates.
—Deuteronomy 6:4–9

One of the most important things you will ever do as a parent is to build open, continuous and heartfelt spiritual communication in your family. This is the spiritual conversation that threads its way through all of our interactions with each of our kids. It is the weaving of biblical teaching into the very fabric of our family life and our children's hearts. This is the kind of teaching Jesus did with his disciples, who were "with him" (Mark 3:14) almost constantly for three years. This is the great thing about being in a family—we are together in the living of life for many years. God intends that we take this opportunity to impart spiritual training to the minds and hearts of our kids. And the primary way we do that is as we go about our normal activities.

For Geri and me, this came as a relief. If we had depended on scheduled times to teach our kids about God, we would have been overwhelmed. Family devotionals and discipling times were essential, but most of our teaching was done during our normal routine: meal times, riding in the car, doing odd jobs around the house, hanging out, relaxing, playing and conversing.

As you go through the day, apply the Bible to situations you and your kids encounter. Bring it in naturally. Show how God and his word relate to life—to everything from the beauty of creation to the ups and downs of human experience. Don't change your voice into a sanctimonious "holy tone" when you mention the Bible! Don't limit your conversational references to Scripture to those times when you are correcting or disciplining the children.

When we impart spiritual truths in this way, kids function better and learn more readily. They see that walking with God is real and not reserved for the super-religious. They see that Jesus is not to be compartmentalized into a segment of our life; he is our life.

Family Worship

Some of your most effective, inspiring and enjoyable times in building your family will be during those special occasions of family worship. Gathering the family together to sing, pray, study the Word and share your hearts will form some of your most precious family memories.

Family devotionals take some planning and imagination. They require creativity. We also need to be realistic. Families with young children have to adjust to the attention span of little ones, yet they need to learn to sit quietly and respectfully as we sing, talk and pray. We suggest setting a once per week time for this, preferably just after dinner. Make it a time to enjoy singing, to pray together, to read the Bible and to talk about some basic Bible concepts. Topics can range from discussing the greatness of God to telling and acting out the great Bible stories we know and love.

The most important goals are to make these times fun, energetic and real, and to really get in there with God's word to address needs. When you do that, household worship becomes a cornerstone of your family life.

Let us close by saying again that of all the concepts we seek to impart in this booklet, Family Spirituality is one of the most important. As much as any of us might wish it, there is no guarantee that our kids will grow up and follow us into the faith. But one thing that will make this more likely is when we have a genuinely spiritual family. Hypocrisy in parents can disillusion kids and kill their faith—and so can functioning on an external level with them. But if we as parents are spiritual, and if we build our family accordingly, the chances of our children one day choosing to follow the Lord are much increased. May we live our lives from the inside out, and may we teach our children about God—from our hearts to theirs!

Group Discussion Questions

- How is the daily prayer going between you and your spouse? Is it becoming a regular habit?

- How are you doing as a family praying together? What are some ideas that have worked for you?

- Do you feel that your family easily and readily discusses spiritual topics? Do the kids feel free to ask you questions?

- How can you make spiritual conversations a regular part of your family life?

- Do you have consistent times of worship and Bible study as a family? How is it going?

- What are some especially effective family devotions that you have done together?

My Daily Steps to a Stronger Family

Principle 8: **Family Spirituality**

*Acknowledge and **take to heart this day** that the LORD is God in heaven above and on the earth below. There is no other. Keep his decrees and commands, which I am giving you today, so that it may go well with you and your children after you and that you may live long in the land the LORD your God gives you for all time.*

—Deuteronomy 4:39–40, emphasis added

Day One (day) _____ (date) _____:

Read Principle 8: **Family Spirituality** Study and Group Discussion Guide.

Take some time to think about and reflect upon your spiritual life and its impact on your family.

- Do you feel that you are living your Christian life from the inside out? Is your heart where it needs to be?

- How do you feel about the example you are setting for your family in this area? Are you close to God, walking daily with him, talking to him in prayer, listening to his word in personal Bible study? Do you have a time set aside for your daily spiritual devotions?

- Discuss with your spouse or a close spiritual friend the status of your personal walk with God. Get their input, and make any decisions you need to in order to be able to build your family from an "inside out" position.

Day Two (day) _____ (date) _____:

Read Deuteronomy 6:4–9.

Note the verse that says that God's commandments are to be upon our hearts, and then we are to impress them on our children.

- Why is the order (on our hearts, impress them on our kids) important? What difference does it make in our ability to build a spiritual family that the word of God is first on our hearts as parents?

- Write down some reasons below:

_____

_____

_____

Day Three (day) _____ (date) _____:

Read Philippians 4:6; 1 Thessalonians 5:16–18; Ephesians 6:18.

Note the phrases "in everything," "pray continually" and "on all occasions." Let's take a closer look at our family's spiritual life.

- What do these phrases tell you about the nature of prayer in a family?

- Do you think that this kind of prayer is a part of your family life?

- Do you pray together frequently? Does your family pray together naturally and easily? Do you pray together outside of the "normal" times such as bedtimes and mealtimes? Who usually suggests that you pray?

- Write down some of the occasions or times during the day when your whole family or different family members can pray together. Use your imagination!

_____

_____

_____

Day Four (day) _____ (date) _____:

Reread the section in Principle 8 entitled "Family Prayer."

Note that by "family prayer" we do not intend to limit prayer to times when the whole family is present—different family members can pray together at various times and occasions.

- Have a family devotional about this idea. Study the passages cited in the reading material, and encourage your family to become a "praying family"!

Some ideas for the family devotional:

- Make a family prayer list. Write down some dreams, needs and areas to grow and change in. Come up with some "impossible prayers" that only God can fulfill. Check them off as God answers, and watch your family's faith grow!

- Have family "prayer partners." Have different family members team up to pray at certain times during the week, or agree to have a "secret prayer" they are laying before God just between the two of them.

- Pray at unexpected or unusual times; pray spontaneously. Begin this week in your family to pray on the spot, at the moment. These do not have to be long prayers, nor do they have to take place in a private setting—just start praying together more frequently and make it natural, real and fun.

Day Five (day) _____ (date) _____:

Read the section in Principle 8 entitled "Family Bible Study and Spiritual Conversation."
Study Deuteronomy 6:4–9.

- There are four settings suggested in this passage in which parents are to discuss scriptural teaching with their children. What are those settings? What do these settings tell you about how God intends parents to teach his word to children? Why is this more effective than restricting Bible discussion to set times such as discipling times or family devotionals?

- How do you think you are doing as a parent (and as parents together) in this area? Are you teaching and explaining the Bible to your kids at home? Are they asking questions? Are you answering them?

_____

_____

- Do you feel that spiritual conversation is a natural and easy part of your family interactions? Is it a difficult or challenging thing for you as a parent to do? How can you make this an ongoing part of your family dynamic? Discuss this with your spouse or another spiritual parent to see how you and your family can progress.

_____

_____

_____

_____

Day Six (day) _____ (date) _____:

Reread the section in Principle 8 entitled "Family Bible Study and Spiritual Conversation."
Study Luke 2:41–52; Deuteronomy 6:20–25.

This week, initiate spiritual conversation at dinner. Here are some sample questions to get you started:

- What is your favorite scripture? Why does it mean so much to you?
- Who is your favorite person in the Bible? What is it about them that inspires and helps you?
- What did you talk about in church Bible class this week? What did you learn?
- What are you learning about God right now?
- Do you have anything you would like the family to pray about?
- Does anyone have a Bible question you have been wondering about?
- For older children: How are your quiet times with God going? Any questions? Do you need any ideas to help make them go better?

Day Seven (day) _____ (date) _____:

Reread the section in Principle 8 entitled "Family Worship."
Plan a time of family worship for your family. Here are some ways to approach your time of planning:

- Plan a time of Bible study and worship that relates to the current needs in the family. This a great time for parents to work together! You can ask the kids some things they would like to talk about or do—older kids can even be given the opportunity to plan a devotional or a section of it. (Note: In addressing needs, be sure not to limit your family devotional times to correcting behavior or attitudes in the children. While it is appropriate to address these kinds of things, the overall direction needs to be encouraging, inspiring and informative.)

- Be sure to consider the ages of the kids. If you have little ones, then the session cannot last too long or be overly intense. If you have a spectrum of ages among the kids, put on your Creativity Cap and do your best to make the devotional an event that everyone in the family enjoys.

- Some topical ideas:

   —Study a Bible character: their strengths, weaknesses, what we can learn.

   —Discuss a parable of Jesus or one of his miracles.

   —Read or act out a Bible story, and then discuss what everyone learned from it.

   —Have a session where the family encourages one another, shares good news and answered prayers, etc.

   —Have a time when everyone opens up about personal needs, requests prayers, etc.

Notes:

_____

_____

_____

_____

_____

_____

_____

_____

_____

_____

_____

_____

_____

_____

_____

_____

_____

_____

_____

_____

_____

_____

_____

_____

_____

Epilogue: **Strong in the Seasons of Life**

When I was a boy in my father's house,
still tender, and an only child of my mother,
he taught me and said,
"Lay hold of my words with all your heart;
keep my commands and you will live."

—Proverbs 4:3–4

These are the commands, decrees and laws the LORD your God directed me to teach you to observe in the land that you are crossing the Jordan to possess, so that you, your children and their children after them may fear the LORD your God as long as you live by keeping all his decrees and commands that I give you, and so that you may enjoy long life. Hear, O Israel, and be careful to obey so that it may go well with you and that you may increase greatly in a land flowing with milk and honey, just as the LORD, the God of your fathers, promised you.

—Deuteronomy 6:1–3

In the future, when your son asks you, "What is the meaning of the stipulations, decrees and laws the LORD our God has commanded you?" tell him…

—Deuteronomy 6:20–21a

At every season of our family's life we must adjust, learn and adapt. New children arrive; they grow up and leave. It can be dizzying, and it flies by. It seems that just as we have figured out one phase, another is upon us. The challenge for us is to go through each of these new stages making Jesus Lord—and enjoying life in the process! We have to keep growing and learning. What worked at one phase does not work at another; what worked in raising one child might not be effective with another.

In our own family, we have experienced change after change. After five years of marriage, *we had our first child*. We had to reinvent our life, and especially did we have to work on keeping our marriage strong, close and exciting. *Then came child number two:* same adjustments as above, but with more energy expenditure. And of course, child number one had to adjust to child number two. Then, just a month after our family had moved to another city, *child number three* arrived. Now, there were more kids in the house than parents! (And oh yeah, we were in a temporary rental at the time, and moved to our newly constructed house months later.) Then, over five years later, unexpectedly (but blessedly!) *child number four* arrived—just after a move to another city. During all these years we went through the "normal" changes of schools and the kids growing and maturing...with a couple more moves thrown in here and there. *Then came college.* With each child's departure we had to pull ourselves together and reinvent our family. *Then they started getting married and having babies.* We even moved into the basement of one of our kids and their family of three for eight months! *Now, after over three decades of raising kids, it's just the two of us again.* I think we're going to check into a rehab clinic.

Change is the great challenge of life. Families that remain strong in the Lord for a lifetime are those that learn the art of mastering change. Or better said, *they learn the art of letting the Master guide them through every change.* It is our observation that families that have not done well spiritually are oftentimes those who have not kept Jesus at the center of their family through times of transition. Somewhere along the way, they lost their grip on the Lord and his plan for their lives. Don't let it happen to you! Resolve, as did Joshua, "But as for me and my household, we will serve the Lord"—for your whole life long! (Joshua 24:15).

Stages of Life in a Family

The stages below are broken down by the ages of children, realizing that the size of your family may mean you are dealing with multiple stages at once. We present the stages in broad strokes to help you see the big picture of family-building over a lifetime.[1]

Stage One: Children Ages Newborn–2 Years Old

Parents are:
- Caregivers and nurturers

---

1. See appropriate chapters in this workbook, or refer to *Raising Awesome Kids—Reloaded*.

- Beginning to train and discipline

Parents, be sure to:
- Keep family priorities centered in the kingdom; maintain strong church attendance, relationships and involvement
- Develop a solid, workable routine: meals, bedtime, etc.
- Renew and deepen your marriage; keep it as top relational priority

Stage Two: Children Ages 2–5

Parents are:
- Caregivers and nurturers
- Increasing the focus on discipline
- Training children's behavior, shaping attitudes
- Teaching children God's word and about the nature of God

Parents, be sure to:
- Establish godly family patterns: strong church involvement, home devotionals and prayer
- Nurture and protect your marriage, keeping it close and intimate
- Establish your authority, secure children's obedience
- Focus on Four Essentials; Love, Obedience, Respect and Honesty[2]
- Begin "natural," ongoing spiritual conversation and teaching (Deuteronomy 6:4–9)
- Learn and implement the concept of reward[3]
- Seek to understand each child's temperament, how to reach and communicate with each one
- Begin shaping and guiding children's friendships

Stage Three: Children Ages 6–11

Parents are:
- Caregivers and nurturers
- Beginning to transition from disciplinarian to trainer and mentor
- Still concerned with behavior, but increasingly focused on shaping attitudes
- Teaching, explaining and applying God's word

Parents, be sure to:
- Build a consistent family schedule: family dinners and devotionals, church attendance

2. See *Raising Awesome Kids—Reloaded,* chapter 5.
3. See *Raising Awesome Kids—Reloaded,* pp. 135–136.

- Keep your marriage close, fun and joyful
- Maintain obedience, but move toward consequences as the preeminent method in discipline
- Establish priority of "seek first the kingdom" over sports, school and homework
- Establish church friends, guiding children to church mentors, "heroes"
- Monitor and guide children's friendships and outside influences
- Help children to develop their own age-appropriate prayer and Bible study habits
- Train work ethic at home and in schoolwork (Colossians 3:23–24)
- Answer questions about faith and life
- Teach children to discipline themselves, do their own homework
- Watch for and respond to beginnings of sexual development
- Assist kids in resolving sibling conflicts, building relationships with siblings
- Build a fun family

Stage Four: Children Ages 12–19

Parents are:

- Caregivers and nurturers with increased focus on helping in thought, emotional and spiritual life
- Teachers, mentors and leaders
- Still disciplining, but with focus on consequences, instruction, admonition and explaining the "why"

Parents, be sure to:

- Keep your marriage close and exciting—kids need to see a great example of married love as they go through their teen years
- Maintain a fun, faithful family as schedule intensifies
- Help them choose good friends
- Show the Bible's relevance to real life
- Build strong relationships in teen ministry and local church
- Help them build good, healthy and righteous habits with Internet, cell phone and social media
- Openly talk through sexual issues; maintain openness
- Prepare them to leave home

Keys in teens coming to the Lord[4]

Parents, be sure to:

- Be vibrant and strong in the faith, inspire them by your example

---

4. See *Raising Awesome Kids—Reloaded,* chapter 16.

- Help them see their personal need for God
- Help them come to their own faith; help them resolve doubts; encourage and welcome their questions
- Help them see through the emptiness of the world, the destructive power of sin
- Help them come to believe in, admire, love and want to follow Jesus

Stage Five: Adult Children, Ages 20+

Parents are:

- Nurturers
- Encouragers
- Advisors (see below)

Parents, be sure to:

- Maintain relationship and communication after children leave home

- Give up control; maintain good influence

- As older children leave home, re-form your family who remain— keep it fun, close and strong

- Guide and advise them as they mature, but allow them to become increasingly responsible for their decisions

- Give younger children preparation and advice as they enter the years of dating and courtship. As your children get older, you have hopefully laid a good foundation of wisdom for them to stand upon as they select a life partner. But remember, your influence for God and for the good remains vital in their lives. Use it wisely.

- Give advice to grown or married children when asked, but do not force your way in. Be caring, involved and available so that they want and ask for your input.

- Plan well in advance for family get-togethers. When the kids are grown and gone, you will have to learn to work with the complexities of increasing numbers of people, and with in-laws. If your family is geographically scattered, it may be wise to choose a "family planner" from among the kids to be sure you schedule occasions to see each other.

Other Changes

Besides the changes that come to a family due to the normal passage of time, there are others as well. Here are a couple of them, and some basic pointers on how to cope.

Moving

Whether we move across town or across the world, our family is affected.

- If you are deciding about a move, remember that your family's spiritual well-being is far more important than career or financial advancement. Ask yourself these kinds of questions: *Would this new move or job put undue pressure on our marriage and family? How is the church situation where we would be moving? Can our family thrive there?*
- As you prepare to move, contact the local church leadership beforehand, and begin building connections well in advance.
- Moving is stressful and disruptive. Be sure to maintain family closeness and prayer during times of transition. Reestablish family routines as soon as possible.
- Use the move as an opportunity to help your children grow. Help them to be patient as they form new friendships. They can learn invaluable lessons during this time about how to give their hearts to new people and how to accept those who are different than they are.

Illness and loss

Illness and loss test families like nothing else. It is vital to stay close to God during these times. As you cope with the illness of friends and family, be sure to explain to kids that while we cannot understand or control what happens, we can trust God to bring good out of it. Prayer for healing is powerful, but we need to help our children understand that God's ways and wisdom are above ours. When you lose a loved one, take the opportunity to teach children about the reality of life and death and about the importance of being anchored to God, who lives forever and does not change. Encourage the children to express what is on their hearts, and help them as they work through their thoughts and feelings.

Group Discussion Questions

- Where are you in the stages of life right now? Give the group a snapshot of where you are as a family.

- Share with the group some valuable lessons you learned as you gained experience in a particular stage. What scriptures helped you the most?

- Is there a particular stage or situation you need help with right now?

- Have you gone through any particular change such as a move or a loss that you would like help with, or about which you can share lessons you learned?

- For those who have seen a child become a disciple, share with the group what made the difference. What scriptures helped the most?

- Those who have seen a child date and marry, share with the group what you learned during the process.

- Grandparents, tell the group how great it is being grandparents, and what the rest have to look forward to. (Keep in mind that we need to finish our group session before too very long!)

My Daily Steps to a Stronger Family

Epilogue: **Strong in the Seasons of Life**

*Acknowledge and **take to heart this day** that the LORD is God in heaven above and on the earth below. There is no other. Keep his decrees and commands, which I am giving you today, so that it may go well with you and your children after you and that you may live long in the land the LORD your God gives you for all time.*

—Deuteronomy 4:39–40, emphasis added

Day One (day) _____ (date) _____:

Read Epilogue: **Strong in the Seasons of Life** Study and Group Discussion Guide.

- What are some of the transitions your family has gone through?
- What scriptures and decisions have helped you most to successfully navigate those transitions?

Day Two (day) _____ (date) _____:

Review in the Study Guide the section entitled "Stages of Life in a Family." Focus on those that are relevant to where your family is at the present time. Read Ecclesiastes 3:1–8.

- What are some of the "seasonal" challenges your family is facing right now?

_____

_____

- Make a list of what you are doing well as you cope with these challenges.

- Make a list of areas where you need wisdom, guidance and strength, and begin praying daily about these needs.

  _____

  _____

Day Three (day) _____ (date) _____:

Briefly review the Study Guide section entitled "Stages of Life in a Family." Examine the stages that are relevant to where your family is at the present time. Read Ecclesiastes 4:9–12; Ephesians 6:18.

- Spend some time talking to your spouse about the stage your family is at right now. Listen attentively to each other as you share together your thoughts and observations.
- Discuss what you are doing right and where you can do better.
- Pray together about your family and your marriage.

Day Four (day) _____ (date) _____:

Read Ecclesiastes 4:9–12, Proverbs 13:20, 17:17, 27:9.

One of the ways we can successfully cope with change and transition is by having other people to help us with their encouragement, advice and wisdom. Yet, as much as we need to do so, opening up with others about our family life may be humbling and can test our ability to trust others.

- Do you have others who consistently help you in your family life? If you already have these people in place, be thankful.
- If not, discuss with your spouse who you would like to invite in to help you with your marriage and child-rearing. Take the time to pray and think about this vital decision, and come together to make it.

Day Five (day) _____ (date) _____:

Read in the Study Guide the section entitled "Other Changes."

- Is your family having to cope with moving, or with illness and loss?
- How do you feel like you are doing? Are you coming through this time with your heart, family and faith intact?

Day Six (day) _____ (date) _____:

Read Luke 2:41–52.

- How does this passage show us some of the challenges of parents and families in transition?

  _____

  _____

- Make a list of the challenges for Mary and Joseph.

  _____

  _____

- List the challenges for Jesus as he transitioned into his teen years.

  _____

  _____

- How did Mary go about helping herself to grow, cope, adapt and learn? (see v. 51b).

Day Seven (day) _____ (date) _____:

In the Study Guide, review Stage Five: Adult Children.
Read Deuteronomy 4:9–10; Psalm 71:17–18, 78:5–6.

People from a generation ahead have much to offer to those following behind. Their hard-won experience is invaluable to those who are in the midst of battles and challenges they have already experienced. This is the special value of grandparents and of older people in our life.

- Do you have older, experienced people who are available to help and encourage you and your family?
- If you do, be sure to invite them into your family life so that you will benefit from their godly influence.
- If you do not, think and pray about finding those who could be this for you and your family.
- If you are already in the Adult Children stage, realize that you have much to offer those families who are coming behind you. Pray for God to use you to help others. Remember: It is not that you did everything perfectly—it is your experience and faith that are desperately needed. Make yourself available to younger families and parents, realizing that your influence and involvement can be invaluable.

Notes:

_____

_____

_____

_____

_____

_____

_____

_____

_____

_____

_____

_____

_____

_____

_____

_____

_____

_____

_____

_____

_____

_____

_____

_____

_____

_____

_____

_____

_____

Notes:

Books from Sam and Geri Laing

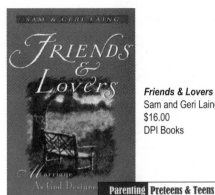

Raising Awesome Kids–Reloaded
Sam and Geri Laing
$15.00
DPI Books

Friends & Lovers
Sam and Geri Laing
$16.00
DPI Books

The Wonder Years
Sam and Geri Laing
Elizabeth Thompson
$13.00
DPI Books

The Guilty Soul's Guide to Grace
Sam Laing
$13.00
DPI Books

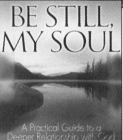

Be Still, My Soul
Sam Laing
$13.00
DPI Books

A Life Worth Living
Geri Laing
$13.00
DPI Books

Mighty Man of God
Sam Laing
$12.00
DPI Books

The Tender Years
Geri Laing and
Elizabeth Thompson
$14.00
DPI Books

All available for purchase at www.ipibooks.com

Sam and Geri Laing

The Essential

8

PRINCIPLES OF A
GROWING MARRIAGE

An Eight-Week Discussion Series for Married Couples

What is The Essential 8: Principles of a Growing Marriage all about?

Simply put, this is a hands-on workbook to help you get your marriage on a solid spiritual foundation and keep it there. It is an eight-week plan designed for individual study on a daily basis, and in a small discussion group once per week. Here are the eight principles that will be covered:

The First Principle: **Jesus Is Lord**
The Second Principle: **Know Yourself, Know Your Spouse**
The Third Principle: **Communicate: Clearly and Kindly**
The Fourth Principle: **Husbands: Love and Lead**
The Fifth Principle: **Wives: Admire and Adapt**
The Sixth Principle: **Solid Stewardship**
The Seventh Principle: **Hot and Holy**
The Eighth Principle: **Love for a Lifetime**

Workbook: $10.00 (Bulk discounts available)
2-Hour DVD: $10.00 (Bulk discounts available)

Illumination Publishers International

For the best in Christian writing and audio instruction, go to the Illumination Publishers International website. We're commited to producing in-depth teaching that will inform, inspire and encourage Christians to a deeper and more committed walk with God. You can reach our office at (832) 559-3658.

www.ipibooks.com